Family Road Tripping without Falling:

How to Survive and Thrive with your Kids on the Road

BY ROSA AND BENJAMIN OVADIA

Motivational**PRESS**®
LEADERS IN GLOBAL PUBLISHING

Published by Motivational Press, Inc.
1777 Aurora Road
Melbourne, Florida, 32935
www.MotivationalPress.com

Manufactured in the United States of America.

ISBN: 978-1-62865-415-8

Contents

To Daniel and Ella, our favorite travel buddies.

Introduction

HAVE YOU EVER IMAGINED being able to see the United States with your kids without them resenting you or each other when you return home? What if you could complete an entire week's vacation for less than the cost of two round trip airfares across the country? What if your kids would be asking you when the next trip would come? What if they would bring their travel knowledge into their classrooms to the awe of their teachers?

The logistics and constraints of a modern family are perhaps more challenging than ever. In planning a big road trip, families have asked us: Can we do it with our limited vacation time? Can we make it with our limited budget? Can we do this with limited patience for kids fighting or complaining? Will the kids (and we) get enough sleep to enjoy this? Will we see enough and remember what we did on the road? Can we drive far enough and long enough to see the other side of the country and have extraordinary family bonding time (we get so little)? The answer is Yes! We will show you how you can bond, enjoy and retain vivid memories of the best travel you have ever had; not someday, but now.

We are a middle-class family of four: Rosa and Ben (30-somethings), Danny and Ella (both under 11). As parents, we both work full-time during the week, volunteer at the PTA, visit family, take the kids to their various sports and activities, and find our free time melting away. We wanted to find a way to spend some real quality time with our kids, and each other, before the kids grow up to realize we are not as cool we tell them we are.

A few years ago we started taking short road trips around the east coast. The most important thing we discovered was how much fun we had on the drive. The drives became an excellent time to talk, catch up, and get to know each other. When we got home, we had great stories to tell and share with family and friends. As time went on, we drove farther and spent more time in the car together. After a couple of longer trips to Niagara Falls and Savannah, we decided it was time to discover the rest of the country in our Honda Civic.

As of today we have traveled to every state accessible by car and have developed an expertise when it comes to the family road trip. We have travelled to 49 states and 1 Canadian province in 2.5 years, driving over 40,000 miles on 72 carefully-planned travel days (including weekends, of course). We did all of this without breaking the bank, a smaller investment than the beachside vacations or week-long Disney trips we could have taken instead. We learned a lot on the road and have many tips, stories and hidden gems to share. Ride along with us and plan your own travel with your kids as you go!

Chapter 1

Planning the Journey

"Not All Those Who Wander Are Lost."

— *J.R.R. Tolkien, The Fellowship of the Ring*

THE ULTIMATE DESTINATION of your road trip can determine the flavor and texture of your journey. We like to name our various adventures according to this ultimate destination. Seattle, Texas, California and Washington D.C. all became battle cries for us as we headed out in our little Honda Civic. Each time, we were determined to place another pin in our oversized United States map (mounted on a styrofoam board at home) and to add another story to tell our friends when we got back to home base.

Once we decided to conquer the United States as a family, we wanted to have a map and put colored pins in it to commemorate, and keep track of, our adventures. These maps are available for sale, complete with beautiful frame and coordinated, colorful pins. The packaged maps are quite pricey, however. A trip to Staples will save a great deal of money, and still give you the same, satisfying feeling when you press a pin into your latest state. Depending on your family road trip goals, a map of either kind may be a perfect, vibrant motivator in your home. It worked for us on our way to our 49th state!

The first step in choosing a destination is considering how many days you have available to take the trip, the time of year, and what type of attractions your family would most like to see along the way. To visualize your trip routes, the oversized pin map is a good tool. We have limited vacation time so we like to plan our trips around holidays and long weekends. School breaks and summer vacations are also ideal for road trips, since we do not have to worry about the kids missing school.

The constraints of a modern family are significant. There are kids' activities (our older boy likes soccer and baseball and now plays 3 instruments, while our younger girl is an actress and loves play dates). We try to avoid the kids missing school. Our little ones are still at an age where they feel missing school is something you just do not do, and we like to encourage this type of thought for as long as we can. Even taking the kids out of school early for a doctor appointment leads to little-person judgment and scorn.

Work allows us some flexibility, but limited days are even more limited when time must be taken for a dentist or doctor checkup or even sometimes-quirky days off school. If you are going to do a lot of family travel as we have, you must guard the days off carefully and this means, generally, we parents do not go to doctor appointments or even some kids' activities together. One of us has to fill in the other so we do not miss out. So if we can scrounge together maybe 6 working days (and add two weekends around these days)—we're off to a hard-won 10-day adventure. We have crossed the country and come home in just over a week, and have traveled furthest north and furthest south on the east coast on a three day weekend (as far as Maine and Florida).

You want to consider weather conditions during the time of year you are traveling, in the region you are exploring, when choosing a destination. Traveling across Colorado at the end of December will find you traveling precariously up (or worse, down) a mountain waiting for snow drifts to clear so you can see the road. You may even have to reroute your trip when several roads are blocked by an avalanche.

The intermediary attractions along the way to your ultimate destination fuel the excitement of the trip, as well as enhance the total experience. Are you a nature-loving or hiking family? You might want to stop and explore a few national parks along the way. Do you like historic locations or maybe art museums? There will be many of these to choose from on your trip. Among the four of us, we each have our own ideas about where we want to go and what we want to see. Each of our preferences have been considered during our road trips.

A good place to start is to go to TripAdvisor.com and figure out what lots of other people think are the best places to go—in aggregate, they really know best. TripAdvisor is powerful collective wisdom, especially the feature we use the most: Things to Do. Imagine you want to put a pin in the map in Mississippi. You want to go to a top attraction, one that is close to the major roads you will take to get there. So, do you want to ask a few friends that have some experience in the state, or millions who have already been there?

TripAdvisor lets you ask the millions of users and get detailed reviews on why a certain attraction got a 5-star rating (or at least close). Most times, we have taken the recommendations and have not been disappointed. One time in Biloxi, Mississippi, the top attraction was a rest stop, though. Even the reviewers were careful to note this was not really an attraction, just a well-done pit stop. We kept sifting through the reviews until we found a N.A.S.A. engine testing facility to see instead. Remember, your family will have its likes and dislikes and we are not a "rest stop attraction" family, it turns out.

A fun way to get the kids involved in choosing and getting excited about the intermediary destination points is to have them do their own research. One of our trips took us through Memphis, Tennessee, as well as Hannibal, Missouri. We chose Graceland as our destination in Memphis, and Mark Twain's boyhood home and museum in Hannibal. In this case, we assigned one location to each one of the kids and had them research the destination and people involved. Each child then gave us a short presentation of their findings.

When we got to each location, we had our little personal tour guides to show us around. The places became even more exciting to the kids and the research they did made these tourist attractions come alive for them. The experience was enhanced for us as well when our little tour guides pointed out the different things they recognized from their research at home.

Thinking back to our Memphis trip, one of our most interesting experiences was then 6-year-old Ella researching "the King" and taking us through some of the highlights of Elvis' life story. She became fascinated by Priscilla and started to research her as well. When you let kids loose on the internet, though, do not be surprised when the innocent question "what's a fair?" becomes a longer conversation about "what's an affair?" In fairness to the process, we explained the distinction to our little girl. We are raising kids that ask the tough questions—even if they are surprised to learn how tough their innocent questions really are.

Your family, like ours, will have likes and dislikes in experiences, learning and attractions. Ask the kids, they will let you know. How does a New York cave with an underground boat ride sound (the Howe Caverns tour is a fantastic experience, by the way)? Would you rather see an 18th century village in Urbandale, Iowa or the Michigan State Fair? Would you rather sleep in and watch Nickelodeon or leave early to book it to Great Sand Dunes National Park in Colorado (they have sand sledding, you know)? Research is not just for adults, let the kids give it a whirl and give them a real say in your travels.

In our family, we have each chosen a destination and it has been a powerful way for each of us to own a trip. We chose our own sites for different reasons, but a part of each reason was aspirational—to see something truly wonderful and to see it together, to learn about it together, to get there (and back) as a family with stories to share. Each trip must be planned for the enjoyment of both kids and adults.

A museum-hopper tour of children's museums will not motivate the adults to persevere through nights of limited sleep or the heavy driving days. Similarly, fine art or architecture alone will not keep the kids engaged in a cross-country odyssey. There has to be a mix of child-friendly and adult-friendly stops, where learning and experience can be had on multiple levels. The good news: you can do this anywhere and it does not take a ton of planning to get you on the road with a good plan. So where have you not visited that you want to experience with your kids? This is the question we ask as a family and we listen to our two under-11 kids to give them ownership and shared power over our limited time to explore together before they are off to college, before they have families of their own.

Our first questions are: can we get there by car with the time that we can budget away from work and school? Can we have amazing experiences that we will remember and discuss for the time we will have before our next trip (in our case, figure in 2-4 months)? Can we plan day-by-day stops that will create both intense experiences and a running narrative of our exploration through geography and time? What will make this trip memorable and can we stick the landing like Olympic gymnasts?

The first cross-country road trip we took as a family was to Seattle. The decision to go there stemmed from several reasons. The leading reason was our decision to drive to every state we could; this trip would add many new states to our collection and many pins to our map. The fact that we had the time to drive to the west coast and back was another reason we decided to go. The route was planned around one particular intermediary destination Rosa wanted to see: Mount Rushmore. Choosing Mount Rushmore led to adding Yellowstone, which is not far and still on the way to Seattle. The rest of the intermediary stops of this trip were found by searching for suggestions online on sites like TripAdvisor and a collection of blogs.

One of our shorter trips over a long weekend was to Quebec City. This trip started when our youngest found out there was something called an Ice Hotel somewhere in Canada. Her teacher mentioned this location in the classroom and Ella just had to go and see it. Rosa went online and found the Ice Hotel was closing for the season in just a few weeks; with this quickly-gathered information, a destination and a timeframe were chosen.

The intermediary destinations ended up being just as wonderful as the magnificent Ice Hotel built entirely of ice and snow in Quebec, Canada. We stayed in a delightful little hotel in Quebec City, tried the traditional French cuisine and strolled through the streets of the old city at night. The next day we went to the Olympic Park in Montreal and took in the view from the Montreal Tower, the tallest inclined tower in the world. We also discovered a superb fast food chain called Tim Horton's. We stopped at several of these along the way, enjoying chocolate-filled cookies and delicious soups and sandwiches, all ordered in Ben's high school-level French from decades back.

Not all destinations have to involve a day's worth of hours in the car. When Ben wanted to take the kids to Washington D.C., we added Colonial Williamsburg to the itinerary. After a quick email to our Congressman, we were given passes to tour the White House, planned a 10-mile stroll through downtown D.C. monuments and museums, and the entire trip fell into place.

Our most recent cross-country trip destination was Alaska. This was our most ambitious trip from the start. Initially, we had some vacation time saved up and a plan, but we hesitated. In order to drive from New Jersey to the Alaskan highway and get back in time we would have had to drive nonstop for several days. We told the kids we were rethinking our destination, since we felt it would not be safe to drive through unknown Canadian and Alaskan wilderness with very little sleep. Rosa also read a blog which stated it is a good idea to carry bear spray when traveling down the Alaskan highway. Bears, unknown wilderness and exhaustion just did not make for a good plan.

This was the trip where planning ended up deciding our route most of all and began as a challenge from our little boy or, rather, disappointment. We realized in 11 days, we could not get to Alaska solely by car. It would mean day after day of driving, half a day in Alaska and the same grueling return trip—and that is if all went well. Plus remember, bears. We decided this trip plan could not work. "You mean we're not going to Alaska?" asked a wide-eyed Danny.

Back to the drawing board; surely, there was a way. Wherever you want to go, however ambitious, do the math and you will find your route. We ended up taking a road trip to Los Angeles, hopping a couple of flights to Juneau and a couple of flights back (because this was by far the cheapest airport to fly from, especially with the Seattle layover each way) and put an epic road trip around the flights. The math worked and we executed to plan with a few additions and a few subtractions along the way.

When planning an 11-day trip over 6,000 miles, the math might seem reasonable. It works out to approximately 600 miles per day, which is manageable. At an average speed of, say, 60 miles per hour—that is 10 driving hours per day. But that is not the reality of the road trip for a few reasons.

One, we want to make stops. Some of the stops along our Los Angeles road trip en route to Alaska could have easily been a 2-3 day adventure to take in all the sights and attractions. We would average closer to 4 hours per car stop. Disneyland is a full day, at least 8 hours; knowing us it would be closer to 10. Our flight schedule told us 26 hours in Juneau, but the flights themselves take time (maybe 12 hours including layovers). So take all that time out—roughly 76 hours of attractions and flying time—and you have 3 fewer days to drive. Take those 3 days out and you have to drive 750 miles per driving day. So that is possible with 12.5 hours of driving for each driving day.

Two, we need to sleep. We still remember an earlier road trip where sleeping was fitful and frustrating. **Important tip—remember to sleep and plan for it nightly.** For the kids, the car becomes a traveling bed (and we make sure to bring pillows and blankets), but for the adults it is not the same. It does not have to be pretty, but putting your head on a pillow in a stationary bed is a necessity given the sheer velocity and perseverance required to complete a trip like we had planned to Alaska.

Three, you have to eat. We have done some experimentation with coolers, portable ovens and mounds of snacks. For this trip, we kept the snacks, but avoided road cooking or cooling. It would be drive-thru for some meals, but for some we would need to get out of the car and sit down. Sanity, sometimes recaptured in a sit-down restaurant, is a real factor for a long road trip.

Those are some points to keep in mind, but you do not take a road trip with your kids just because the logistics can work. That said, the logistics do need to work. Otherwise, you do not find the success that an investment in a big road trip requires.

One of our top recommendations is to make sure that the logistics work day-wise with the 24 hours per day that you get; that is why we decided not to car-trip to Juneau and back—the math did not work out. It turns out another fact we did not know when planning that would have been helpful: Juneau is not reachable by car. So our route ended up being the only way to arrive at our intended capitol destination, with adventure on the way to and from and without taking a cruise ship that we could not afford (either time-wise or financially).

Sometimes you choose your destination and sometimes, because of the constraints involved, it chooses you. Where do you want to go and what do you want to see along the way? Consider how much time you have, the time of year and what you want to see to choose your own adventure. Once you have your destination in mind, it is time for research. A map of some kind, either physical or virtual is a must so you can conceptualize a there-and-back trip and that is helpful on the macro level.

But on the micro level, truth be told, Siri (or generally, phone GPS) is much more helpful. Why? Because wherever you want to go, it is not a straight line. You need to take certain routes for a major trip, usually highways. Once you zoom in on GPS, you realize that highways take you through certain cities and towns and you do not want to go too far off of the beaten path. If you do go off the path, you can find yourself 2,000 miles from home driving 25 miles per hour over a long stretch of road. Do that for too long and it most likely does not get your family there-and-back in time.

Open GPS, zoom in, and start writing down the towns and cities that are on, or just off, the path. **Important tip for GPS— make sure the destinations are your intended ones.** One of the four times we missed Four Corners National Monument (in Colorado, Arizona, Utah and New Mexico all at once) had a lot to do with the fact that "Four Corners" is part of the name for many, many spots in Colorado. The first "Four Corners" we chose was about 200 miles off target.

A few notes about iPhone's Siri. First, she has a great default voice, but she can be adapted to different dialects and languages and, with a flip of a setting, can even become a he. Siri is also a know-it-all, but if she cannot understand you as you speak, tap on the screen that displays whatever she understood and manually change the text so she gets you what you need. As relates to travel, Siri is the ultimate in inspiration. She does not sweat the small stuff like sleep time or meal time or even gas in the tank; she pushes you on your journey with the most optimistic of time predictions. And that can be powerful.

Go ahead, ask Siri "Directions to [the furthest place you can imagine getting to by car in the United States]"—she will get you there. We love to play around with Siri to get inspiration; she makes the far-off places seem possible. Coast-to-coast in 2 1/2 days? Why not, add a full day and you can actually pull it off.

Another option for mapping out your route involves Google Maps and a sheet of notebook paper. Find the addresses of each intermediary location on your trip and type the first two into Google with the word "to" between the addresses. Google will give you an approximate distance and time between them. Next make a list of every location and the time to get from one to the next. This gives you a picture, with a running time log, of the entire trip. We just recently planned a road trip that will span nearly 3,000 miles over 4 days and this is what our initial itinerary looks like:

Leave New Jersey 4/13 at night.

Brunch in Nashville, Tennessee - Gaylord Opryland Resort on 4/14. [12 hours]

Get a hotel near Murfreesboro, Arkansas 4/14 at night. [7 hours]

Murfreesboro, Arkansas - Crater of Diamonds (Mine) on 4/15 morning. [0 hours]

Hot Springs, Arkansas - Buckstaff Bathhouse on 4/15 afternoon. [1.5 hours]

Get a hotel near Little Rock, Arkansas 4/15 at night. [1 hour]

Little Rock, Arkansas - Heifer International (Village) on 4/16 morning. [0 hours]

Get a hotel 2 hours out of Lewisburg, West Virginia on 4/16 night. [10 hours]

Lewisburg, West Virginia - Lost World Caverns on 4/17 morning. [2 hours]

Arrive in New Jersey on 4/17 night. [7 hours]

Consider how many hours you want to be on the road. Factor in bathroom, food, and gas stops. Ask yourself: is this achievable? If not, it is time to rework the trip itinerary.

Not all meals need to slow you down. There are.many options for meals on the go, and not all of them have to be cold or simple sandwiches. We will detail more on food later. Remember that you will need to sleep. Time is important, so at this early stage of planning you can block off the day-by-day which gets you home in time to return to school and work. You have a skeleton trip and with this alone you can get on the road because—more good news—you can take the internet with you.

We do not recommend booking motel/hotel rooms ahead of time (or campsites for that matter), see where the road takes you and use your phone to search and book hotels on the way. One of our worst road experiences was leaving Memphis exhausted, but having to get ourselves to a booked room in Dallas that evening. That was just a painful 6 hour drive and there was too much temptation to give up the paid hotel night (which we did not, but paid the price in sheer exhaustion).

Put the time you plan on leaving home at the beginning of your written route. Now add your calculated travel time and you will be able to figure out approximately what time you will be at your various destinations. This will show you how many days you need for your route. You might discover your original route might be too ambitious or not ambitious enough. In either case, you will have a virtual, timed map of your road trip and you will be able to adjust if necessary. There are several websites that will give you your most efficient route if you just plug in your initial, intermediary, and final destinations. AAA.com, MapQuest.com and RandMcnally.com are good, user-friendly examples.

Is the trip manageable? At this high-level stage, we are concerned with what is possible. Can we get enough sleep? How many driving hours per day will make this trip work? Does the time of year make sense (do not drive into snow going out west without four-wheel drive or tire chains, or really at all)? Can we agree on a trip plan with rest stops, sleep stops and attractions that will engage us, teach us something and push our limits just a bit? Are the kids doing their part to choose the adventure? Think backward: if we get to the final stop and all the stops before and after, will this trip be a memorable adventure or a painful part of a future therapy session? Think it through and remember that enjoying a road trip begins with the initial plan for success that you come up with as a family.

Getting Your Family on the Road/ Getting the Kids Involved

1. It is time for a family meeting. We prefer to have our official family meetings at one of our favorite family-friendly restaurants. Dinner at home has too many distractions for us. One of us is running back and forth

putting food on the table, bringing seconds, clearing and cleaning. Eating out gives us all a chance to relax, sit around a table and focus on each other. This is a great time to put away the cell phones and talk to your kids about an upcoming adventure. In the beginning, the kids do not have original ideas, but even early on they will have opinions about your ideas.

2. Share power at this early stage and start planning a road trip. Do not bite off a cross-country trip the first time, start smaller. Have a few destinations in mind and engage the kids; have it be their choice (among the options you provide) what the first adventure will look like. Look around the table for possible visual aids. Ben loves using sugar packets to symbolize the different states and their geographic relation to one another. He likes to show the kids a little geography with these handy packets as he maps out what a 3-5 day excursion might look like. We occasionally access our Google maps at this stage, but no checking email or texts.

3. Make assignments and set some soft deadlines. You will all emerge from this first meeting with a basic plan in mind (at least, when you are taking the trip) and lots of potentials to think about, but your first plan will not always work. You do not know where the conversation will go and so, instead of doing hours of research ahead of time, assign the research at the family meeting.

4. The parents do the heavy lifting in preparation to get on the road. Consult TripAdvisor and map out the day-by-day whatever direction you are going. Do not plan more

than 8 hours of car travel per day in your first attempt. What are the major cities you will be passing by and what are the top attractions? Are there National Parks to consider or famous museums or interesting restaurants? Who is going on this trip—just the parents and kids, or is an aunt or grandparent going to be a travel companion as well?

5. Get the gang together again; this meeting can be at home with a laptop or desktop computer handy. List what you have found in the direction you chose—would you rather the A or B attraction? Get consensus. If you need to Google-search A and B for detail, do it. It is easy at this stage to thumbs-up a destination or scratch it entirely from memory.

6. The process puts the kids in the driver's seat with you. In 3-5 days, you may have 4-8 stops; let the kids each research at least one stop and give you their input. If the stop centers around a person, a speedy Wikipedia biography should quickly give your little one some ownership. When the kids are small, you can read the bio to them and have them take some cute notes or even draw a few pictures.

7. Time for a pre-trip meeting between the adults. We like to have virtual meetings between us where we send ideas for the trip and feedback on these ideas by emails back and forth for a few weeks. Sometimes this is done during a lunch hour at work, sometimes at the end of the day.

8. The trip is eventually planned day-by-day and has logistics that only grownups find important spelled out.

What time are we leaving (when do we need to get home from work)? What are we doing each day? Where are we sleeping and when? What are we taking with us? Are we visiting any friends or relatives and, if so, when? What is our basic budget? What are the priority destinations (these are destinations that you would spend an extra hour in if at all possible and that you absolutely do not want to miss)? Who do we have to notify that we are leaving (school, neighbors, family, work) and have we filled out the forms and sent the requisite text messages or emails?

9. Print out what you absolutely need, but feel free to rely on emailed notes. If you have booked rooms, have the confirmations in your email. Any pre-booked attractions, same thing, keep these on hand in easily-accessible phone email. Take any discount cards that you have (AAA, student, military, etc.), at least one credit card, a driver's license for each driver, fully charged phones and all the charging plug-ins. Pack your car as neatly as you can, it will not stay that way for long. You can buy anything you have missed in your packing (national chains and local rest stops are all the insurance you really need).

10. Put away any lingering doubts; you really need to get on the road. Just go and let the adventure begin!

Chapter 2

Budgeting Your Adventure

"It's money. I remember it from when I was single."

— *Billy Crystal*

THE TOP CONCERN for many families considering a long road trip is the funding required to complete the journey. Issues of budget may be among the top trepidations before leaving on a trip. As a family, we came to choose driving adventures in the United States largely as a result of budget constraints.

We always knew we liked the adventure of travel and thought our longer travel would turn into European vacations, or cruises, or plane rides to far-away destinations. The problem was that we could not and still cannot afford these. If you open up your favorite travel booking app (we are still partial to Expedia and Travelocity, but any similar site will do) try some experimenting. If we decided to travel to Hawaii, for instance, we are looking at $1,000/round trip airline ticket per person and $150-300/night in a hotel. A four-night vacation to Hawaii, then, would cost us over $5,000.

The cost of certain vacations fluctuates during different seasons. Prices are higher during peak seasons and lower during off-peak seasons. These constraints would be less of a problem if not for the fact the kids are usually in school during the off-peak seasons. Perfect example: we just took a look at cruises leaving from Florida. They are affordable when the kids are in school (off-peak) but plan for the winter vacation and they are triple the cost. You will notice in your own experimentation on travel sites that travel in the beginning of December is likely far less expensive than at the end of December (when kids are off of school nationwide). You could consider pulling the kids out of school during the off-peak times of year, but if your kids are anything like ours they will protest missing the time.

It is worth the time, however, to price out these other vacations involving sea and air because that is where the magic of road trip travel starts: it is affordable when compared to these other options. It is not that we could not save up and spend four days a year in Hawaii, though this would stretch us significantly. But, in comparison, we could travel for three weeks of the year by car, explore amazing destinations all over the United States and have the family bonding time we have come to cherish for the same investment. It is this consideration that has left us with 49 states under our belt and no immediate plans to reach Hawaii for a complete 50.

The starting point of budgeting a family road trip with kids, then, is to consider the more expensive options. Any road trip destination will be affordable in comparison and you want to choose an approximate dollar amount to spend. For us, $5,000 on a single trip is out of reach, but if we plan a trip that is exciting enough, we will consider an investment of $2,500 - $3,500. For four travelers, this is not bad for a 10+ day excursion, though we will typically only take one of these per year.

A financial reference point in our minds is a beachside vacation we could take in our home state of New Jersey. Spending time at the beach, or "down the shore" as New Jersians like to refer to it, is a go-to vacation for many families who live in our region. In peak season, the beach house alone will cost you in the neighborhood of $3,000 for seven days. We tried this once and, though we all had a pretty good time, we decided once was enough for us. We prefer a less stationary vacation and, for the same time and expense, we can enjoy the beach on the west coast for a few days with a few great stops along the way.

When you consider an airplane ride or a cruise, remember you are paying per person. This is very different in the car where you spend the same amount no matter how many travelers are riding (as long as they can fit in a single car). For us, this means 4-5 passengers are sharing the single gas cost. Gas is the first budget item to consider in budgeting your family road trip with kids. When you have planned your trip day-by-day and stop-by-stop, you will have an idea of the mileage you are considering.

Coast-to-coast is approximately 3,000 miles each way, so if we are traveling to the west coast and back, we will add a few miles for detours and consider a total mileage of 7,000. Speaking of mileage, **a travel tip to excite the kids and yourselves is to make sure you record the car mileage when you leave on your trip**. It is a great way to encourage your family on the road and to mark the amazing travel "notches in your belt" on social media posts. We always seem to have at least one Facebook post that says something to the effect of "1,500 miles in the rear view mirror, on Day 2 of our trip we found..."

Remember to take your family car with the best gas mileage on a long trip (any trip longer than 4 travel days) because it will make a huge difference. Our 2012 Honda Civic, with highway driving, gets close to 35 miles per gallon. We love our Honda. Coast-to-coast and back means 20 full fill-ups that will average $35/fill up. So, $700 goes as a line item right into the budget; it is a sunk cost once you decide to leave on your road trip. Compare that to air travel or a cruise for 4-5 passengers, however, and you can marvel at the money you are already saving.

We used to plan travel around hotels. Our thinking was: let us get to somewhere exciting at a nice hotel and the trip will almost make itself. In those days, we spent far more money on hotels than we have in the past few years. If you are traveling to the extreme, you too will find that the nice hotels are almost lost on you because you never really get to enjoy them. We drive as far as we can safely and stop driving before we are too tired to stay awake behind the wheel.

We stop at the hotel to sleep and have breakfast if it is included in the stay, then we continue to our next attraction. A basic, no-frills hotel will run about $55 - $75 per night, depending on the part of the country and time of year you are traveling. **We almost always skip the first evening in a hotel** (we typically leave at 8 p.m. one day and arrive at our first hotel at 10 p.m. or so the following day). As a bonus, night travel tends to avoid major traffic as you set off on adventure. On this long day, we will take turns sleeping in the car to make sure at least one of us is fresh, awake and able to take us toward our destination.

There are two reasons this long day to begin our road trip has become tradition. First, it means the irritability of our kids is reduced. They have no problem sleeping in the car as long as the sun is down and there are pillows and blankets in the back seat. The kids sleep about 10 hours of this journey so their conscious car time is only about 16 hours, with stops to break up any tensions plus their own excitement for the trip to push off any crankiness. Second, taking a full driving day to start your family road trip, you arrive at your first overnight stop with hundreds of miles or more behind you. That is powerful and encouraging because you are far away and well into your adventure on the first day.

On a 10-day trip (with only 8 motel/hotel nights), we are budgeting around $600 for places to sleep with some breakfasts included. We have experienced some awful hotels in our travels, so we will always look at reviews on our Expedia app before booking. Important: do not just look at the hotel stars, they will not tell you the whole story. **Read 4-8 reviews of the hotel you are considering and make out what the reviewers' problems were to figure out if the reasons for the star-deductions are important to your family.**

For us, if a motel/hotel has not been renovated in a long time, it is not likely to affect our night's sleep. **We also always pay attention to whether breakfast is included**; for a family of four on the road, this is a $25 value, so we will factor this perk into our decision of where to stay while still looking for the least expensive option. Figure $50/night without breakfast is equivalent to $75/night with full breakfast included.

We consider, but almost never factor in, exact attraction costs on a trip in advance. We will make mid-trip decisions, however. If we are on an expensive trip, we are unlikely to take the helicopter ride, to buy the professional pictures taken at an attraction, or to go to a fancy restaurant. We will also make sure to consult our National Park Passport (found at National Park Welcome Centers) when traveling to explore a park or two; these are affordable and amazing, bringing the awe factor of a trip up and the average cost of attractions down.

The one destination type where we will consider attraction costs in advance is Disney and other theme parks. We are a walking family. When doing the math for Disney, we can usually see the highlights of any park in a single day (one admission per person). With the high daily cost of admission to the park, we have never spent more than a day at a Disney park on any trip. Frankly, we are not sure what we would have done with a second day in the same park. **By itself, a one-day limit at a Disney park is a huge cost-saving measure.**

For attractions, we will usually budget $100/day and for restaurants, we will usually budget $60/day. Back to the 10-day trip, with the gas ($700), hotels/motels ($600), attractions

($1,000), and restaurants ($600), we are looking at $2,900 total. There are ways to reduce this cost including staying at campsites, packing up to 2 meals per day in advance in the car, focusing on low-cost attractions and so on.

But, **generally, $3,000 for a 10-day road trip (or $300 per day on any trip) is a good reference point.** That figure has proven true for us as a car traveling family of four. An additional family or friend passenger may be a welcome addition for many other reasons, but can also help pay their share (and reduce your own overall cost) of the trip. If this additional passenger is also a licensed driver, you have a third person to shoulder the long hours behind the wheel. In our experience, gas and motel/hotel prices (as long as you all stay in the same room) do not increase with an additional traveler.

The budget for a road trip is also not a decision in isolation from your everyday life. If you are looking to save up for a road trip, reducing expenses at home will help. This may mean going out to eat less often or having staycations during some of the kids' school breaks. If our kids have a four-day break, we are always tempted to plan a travel route, but we will give up several of these every year in order to save up for our bigger trips.

Fundamentally, budget decisions will have a lot to do with what you value, what type of traveling family you are and what limits you are willing to push. We have traveled to Seattle and back to the east coast in nine days. This type of travel is not for everyone, but fewer days will save you money. Truth be told, we usually start with a destination in mind and then figure out how to afford it.

_____

With Alaska, the least expensive option was driving the whole way to and from. That would not work because of time and sanity constraints, so we chose the most inexpensive flights (with layovers each way) from the least expensive airport on west coast. Remember, the goal is to have fun, bond and build memories that you will cherish. You are not on vacation to save money, but expenses of the trip do follow your bank account home.

Thinking of Alaska, Juneau is one destination that is amazingly expensive (it is a cruise ship town). The day trips offered by sites like Viator.com will cost between $120 and $300 per person. This is one reason we decided 26 hours (time for only one day trip) was as much time as we could spend there. The hotels are also quite pricey; only one night was affordable for us on that trip.

We forged ahead with the trip there with a 1-day constraint and maximized this day by booking a Viator.com package deal for each traveler that included a city tour, Mount Roberts tramway and lunch, and a visit to the Mendenhall Glacier. The price was on the lower side for the area—around $125 per person—and created multiple memorable experiences through geology and time. As a trip comparison, on this entire 10-day trip we spent less than the cost of four roundtrip Philadelphia-Juneau airfares alone.

As attractions go, prioritize the "cool" factor. **Paying for memorable experiences and going cheaper on hotels and food will pay off.** Make sure these "cool" sites get family consensus, though. Ben surely wanted to see a Cirque de Soleil show in Las Vegas and Rosa would have loved to take the Vegas train through the Grand Canyon. Cirque de Soleil is pricey and not an attraction Rosa or the kids were interested in seeing. The full day train trip through the Grand Canyon sounded like fun, but would have been expensive and we just did not have the time to devote a whole day to the Grand Canyon on that trip. We all enjoyed walking the city for a few hours, taking in the famous (free) Bellagio water show and catching a medieval jousting tournament at the Excalibur hotel which included a delicious dinner. More family-friendly and a better fit for our collective tastes, the show also was the least expensive of the options. On a family road trip with kids, democracy many times can work.

You will be tempted to purchase souvenirs along the way on your family road trips. The costs of these can vary, depending on the type of attraction and location. Choose a dollar amount ahead of time for incidentals and souvenirs. Keep in mind that your car has limited space. Do you really need to buy that enormous stuffed animal in the shape of a buffalo or can you settle for a small picture on a key chain?

You will find out what kind of traveling family you are as you spend money on your trips. **Take note, record each expense with the date, amount and even assign a category.** You can do this on separate paper or keep your receipts. Another way is to use a single credit card and take a set amount of cash for other incidentals; then record where the cash is spent and use your online credit card statement to download the rest of the expenses.

With a quick Excel document, you can sort your expenses by category and get category totals. This is where your family spends money on vacation so in planning the next trip, take these categories into account and budget the coming adventure. The more you do this scientifically, the more accurate your next forecasts will be. Remember, you will spend money on a road trip with your kids and it does help to have a sense of how much money you will be spending before you pull out of the driveway at home.

Getting Your Family on the Road/ Getting the Kids Involved

1. Check out travel options other than road trips. There are places you have always dreamed of; price them out online. You will get there someday, but the time to experience your family road trips is now because they are by far less expensive than air or sea vacations. See, you are saving money already!

2. For hotels and motels, check out online reviews and remember that these places to stay are not attractions; you are there to sleep. The reviews can tell you pretty quickly if you will have trouble accomplishing that task. Compare hotel night prices among several apps. Considering the size of your family, take into account included breakfast, that is approximately a $25 value each morning.

3. Consider the costs, but build family consensus around which attractions and events you will choose. Share power with the kids because you will not enjoy that expensive opera or fancy restaurant if the kids are giving

you the look that says "I told you I would not like this" the whole time.

4. Take a quick cell phone picture of your odometer. This is your starting point and you will want to do a little subtraction periodically during your trip to announce to the family how many miles you have traveled. This is especially impressive and salient if you check back often enough to announce major milestones like "5,000 miles."

5. Choose your family car with the best gas mileage, the cost savings will add up on a long road trip. Most important is to take a car you are sure will last the journey (newer is usually better). If you are bringing along a family or friend passenger, their car may be the winner of the gas mileage contest.

6. There is nothing better than getting far away from home on the first drive of your trip, adrenaline pumping. We typically drive 26 hours in our first stretch and that's powerful; hundreds of miles from home, you are well on your way to adventure. You also do not spend money on a motel or hotel that first night. If that is too much, however, choose a high mileage mark to drive to and call it a successful first day.

7. Rule of thumb for a family road trip with two kids: budget $300 in expenses per day including gas, places to sleep, attractions, souvenirs and food. Before you get to know your own family travel spending habits, use this as an initial trip budget guide.

8. You do want to know your own family spending habits as you increase road trip vacations with your kids. Track

your spending each day, categorize these expenses and recap the total spending and categorical spending when you get back home. You will have a more accurate idea of the overall trip cost when planning your next trip.

9. When you want to splurge, prioritize amazing attractions that will be memorable over places to stay and spots to eat. You are building memories, so what experiences are worth paying a little extra for?

10. Put away your calculator and take your credit card and some cash, you really need to get on the road. Just go and enjoy the adventure—on budget, we hope!

Chapter 3

Packing for the Road Trip

"All My Bags are Packed and I'm Ready to Go."
— *John Denver, Leaving on a Jet Plane*

A ROAD TRIP DOES NOT MEAN you are heading into the wilderness where nothing is available, where all you have to survive on is what you bring with you. If you forget something, you will have many options for places where you can procure what you need. Still, having what you need with you will save you time on the road, save you money and help keep you on track.

We have, on more than one occasion, ended up far from home in hot weather with no hats. The first time this happened, we were in Florida and planned to spend the next day at Disney World, walking the park. We realized we left our hats at home. Luckily there was a Wal-Mart nearby, and we each got ourselves a fun, touristy, Florida hat. The same thing happened to us on one of our other southern trips. We were in Mississippi and again realized we forgot our hats. Wal-Mart to the rescue again. We now own many, many hats. We just need to remember to take them along.

That said, there are some things that cannot be replaced like your child's favorite book or your favorite sweater. With that in mind, you might consider leaving these irreplaceable items at home. If you forget your favorite item in a hotel or rest stop, it is likely gone forever.

There are some basic categories of items that are useful and necessary on a family road trip with kids. You will need clothing, food, toiletries, medicines if you or your child needs them, vitamins if you or your children take them, a first aid kit, paper towels, and wet wipes. We make sure we both have our phones and chargers with us, as well as several options for entertainment for us and the kids on the road.

There are some items that are more of a luxury, and we decide whether or not to take them along according to the trip that we are embarking on. These items include an electric cooler, hot pot, small portable trucker stove, selfie stick, tablet, and a laptop with an external hard drive loaded with family-friendly television shows and movies. **Whatever you decide to take with you, make sure to make a list and check off the items as you pack your car.** This list can be started as soon as you begin planning your trip. Add and change the list as many times as you want, even while you are packing.

When packing clothing for a trip, remember you always have the option to have your clothes washed at a hotel or to use a local laundromat. We prefer to wash our clothes when we get home and save the time and cost on the road. Since we have limited trunk space and clothing can take up the most room in the car, we have developed an algorithm of sorts (for our family of four) to make sure we always have what we need and do not over-pack.

The first rule of packing clothes is to know how many days you will be on the road. **Pack one bag for every three days on the road.** We have tried several approaches to packing our clothes. We have packed one bag for the adults and one for the kids, but this meant we had to carry two very heavy bags in from the car every time we stopped for the night. We have packed one very large bag with everything, but this was bulky and inefficient.

Packing smaller bags, with clothes for each of us in every bag has worked best for us. Packing in these smaller batches makes finding what you need in every bag so much simpler than packing everything in one or two large suitcases. Each bag should have underwear, socks and tops for each day on the road and no more than two pairs of pants for every three days. Pants tend to take up the most room in the duffle, and wearing the same pair of pants for more than one day without tossing them in the laundry hamper is tolerable, especially on the road. The exception is when you have spilled something which will leave a stain.

When we flew to Alaska, using the small batch packing method meant all we needed to do was grab the bag we had packed especially for that part of the trip. We could leave the rest of our things locked in the car when we left it in long-term parking. We could not take toiletries with us since we would be boarding an airplane and regular-sized shampoo bottles, mouthwash and similar items are prohibited. We decided we would make do with the small, complementary hotel toiletries, even though we do generally prefer to bring our own on road trips. Though most hotels and motels will provide complementary shampoo and even conditioner, you might have a preference for a particular type of hair care product and bringing your own on a road trip is as simple as tossing it into the designated duffle.

You could bring a separate, empty duffle bag for laundry. When you get home, you can take this bag and empty it into your laundry hamper. If you forget to bring this duffle, you can make use of the designated plastic laundry bags hanging in the closets of most hotels and motels. Put your laundry in these bags and toss them in the trunk for washing when you get home.

Pack clothes for sleeping, toiletries, medications and vitamins in a separate, single duffle bag. We pack bathing suits in this duffle as well, in case one of the hotels we choose has a pool and we have some time to splash around. Now when you reach that hotel at 1 a.m., tired from a long day of driving, you can grab one of your clothes bags and your designated toiletries and pajama bag and head into the comfort of your room feeling fully prepared.

Our toiletries suggestions include toothbrushes, toothpaste, mouthwash, dental floss, shampoo, conditioner, razors, shaving cream, liquid soap, luffa, hair brush, and extra hair bands (if one or more of you have long hair). In a pinch, hotel conditioner can replace shaving cream. Do not forget to pack sun block. A sun burn is not a fun thing to experience at any time, but it will feel even worse on the road. Just make sure you put any bottle with liquid in a sealable, plastic bag before tossing it into the duffle bag. This prevents a leaky bottle from making a mess in the inside of your bag and getting a sticky film all over your pajamas.

You have a few options for packing food on the road. There are foods which require refrigeration and those that do not. **If you would like to take perishable foods along, we recommend taking an electric cooler.** This handy machine connects to the lighter socket in the car and keeps foods refrigerated in the back. The cooler comes with an optional adapter that allows the cooler to be plugged into a wall socket when you stop at hotels. Some larger cars have lighter sockets in the trunk, but putting the cooler in the trunk means you need to stop the car in order to prepare meals.

We keep the cooler behind the passenger seat, on the floor. This works for us since Ella is small enough and does not mind having less leg room. You could also place the cooler on the back seat in between the kids, giving each child a designated area which helps prevent the occasional "She's bothering me!" and "He's sitting too close!"

Any dry goods should be stored in paper or plastic bags. This way, when the food is eaten you can simply dispose of the bag at one of your stops on the road. Keep some of the food in the car with you and the rest can be stored in the trunk. We will discuss food options, recipes, and cooking tips on the road in more detail later. Pack a few snacks in a large paper shopping bag and keep it in the back with the kids. That way, the kids can snack when they are hungry and this will keep them satisfied until you are ready to stop for a meal or prepare one on the road.

Have at least one bottle of water per person in the car and keep extra bottles in the trunk. You do not have to buy bottled water for this. Sports bottles are inexpensive and refillable. Many national parks and museums offer water bottle refilling stations. You and the kids will get thirsty on the road and the water is also useful for cleaning sticky faces and hands, as well as heating up in a travel hot pot for soup, tea, and hot chocolate.

Our favorite hot pot memory was traveling through San Juan National Forest in Colorado. It was extremely cold, so cold all of our car windows fogged up and we had to wipe the inside, front windshield every few minutes with our trusty paper towels. We were going the speed limit, around 50 miles per hour, and tension became an extra passenger on this journey. When we fired up the hot pot and enjoyed hot chocolate as a family, things got better. We could even enjoy the beautiful arctic-looking scenery around us as we sipped the hot treat together.

Take some clean, empty plastic bags and always keep one in the car with you. Use these as trash bags and make sure the kids use the bag rather than toss every wrapper and paper cup on the floor of the car. When you stop the car for gas or when you reach one of your destinations, you can toss the full trash bags in a nearby trash can. Without these toss-away bags, driving around in a mobile trash receptacle could put a damper on your road tripping fun.

Keep an empty plastic bag, a roll of paper towels and wet wipes on the front passenger side floor. This does not take up much room, but can be a very useful if there is a spill in the car when you are on the road. We also keep a pack of paper lunch bags in our glove compartment in case one of the kids gets car sick. We have not had to use these bags many times, but when they were needed we were glad to have them. The plastic bag and paper towels came in handy in these situations as well.

A tip for a case of car sickness: first let some air into the car by opening the windows. Sometimes this helps alleviate the situation. If you have the option to pull over and let you child get out of the car and take in some fresh air while stretching his or her legs, this might help as well. If pulling over is not an option and the air from the window is not enough, pass back one of the paper bags (just like an air sick bag on a plane).

If your child gets sick in the bag, put it in the plastic bag, clean up any messes with paper towels and put the paper towels in the plastic bag as well. Tie up the bag and toss it into the next available trash can. Remember those water bottles you have in the car? Make sure your child drinks some water after being car sick. This helps prevent dehydration and will make you child feel better pretty quickly.

Pack a small first aid kit in your trunk, but have a few band-aids, some medicated ointment, and a bottle of pain reliever in the car. Kids and adults can find ways of injuring themselves on the go and it helps to be prepared.

Have each child choose two pillows and a blanket to take with them in the car. We have designated "travel blankets" the kids associate with our travels. If your children have stuffed animals they like to sleep with, these furry creatures should be packed in the car as well. Pack an extra pillow for sleeping in the front passenger seat. The more comfortable you are when it is your turn to sleep, the more rested you will be when it is your time to drive.

Give each child their own "entertainment" canvas shopping bag. Do not pack too many items in these bags, though, or they will end up all over the car before you cross the first state line. Books, notebooks, crayons, and travel games are all great options for these small bags. We keep these canvas bags draped over the front seats so the kids have easy access in the back. You can pack extra items in the trunk if you will be going on a longer trip. Pack a few family-friendly audio books in the trunk, and put one in the car with you. We will discuss entertainment options more in a later chapter.

If you want to pack a selfie stick, keep it handy. Just keep in mind that if you are going to a Disney park, a selfie stick is not allowed. In that case, leave it in the car. If you are not sure if you can bring your selfie stick along to an attraction, consult CanIBringMySelfieStick.com.

If you take a car hot pot with you, keep it on the front passenger side and make sure you have paper cups, spoons, tea bags, hot chocolate packets, and cup of soup packets handy. All of these items will fit nicely in a paper shopping bag or canvas bag by your feet. You can put the roll of paper towels and water in this bag as well. We keep a folding lap top tray in that bag too. Warning: do not keep paper cups uncovered in the back seat at your children's feet; they will end up full of dirt and rendered unusable.

The lap top tray is a handy item found on Amazon.com (where you can find many other small, useful road travel gizmos) that is the size of a small notebook, but folds out into a handy lap tray. We put the hot pot on it while it is heating up rather than keep it on our laps. The lap top tray also comes in handy when preparing sandwiches on the go.

The first time we used the folding tray we were sitting in traffic, driving up to see the Hoover Dam. The wait felt like it would take forever and we were all hungry. We had a loaf of bread, peanut butter and jelly, and a box of plastic spoons in the car. We prepared the sandwiches in the front seat using the folding tray and passed them out to everyone. The roll of paper towels was useful here, because each sandwich was wrapped up to make it easier to eat, and then clean up after. By the time we got to the checkpoint before the Hoover Dam, the hunger was gone and we were ready to explore.

If you choose to take a travel oven with you, pack it in the trunk with a few disposable pans, paper plates and plastic cutlery. A 12-volt travel oven can be purchased online and is great if you want hot food on the road. It will cook a meal and even bake small cakes, but it is better to use it to heat pre-cooked meals. Cooking and baking on the road, though possible, is quite time-consuming.

Put the oven on the folding tray when using it. It will keep the oven stable and protect your lap from spills. You do not need to keep the travel oven in the car at all times, it tends to be bulky. When you are ready to prepare a meal with the oven, find a safe place to stop your car or remember to get it from the trunk before getting into the car after stopping at an attraction or rest stop.

Getting Your Family on the Road/ Getting the Kids Involved

1. "Be Prepared" for your family road trip with kids, as the Boy Scout motto urges. Packing your car with the necessities of the road will mean you have to stop less frequently and you are prepared to recuperate in the car and at the motel/hotel when you are exhausted and maybe even cranky.

2. Start a running packing checklist as soon as you begin planning your route. This is a great way to feel some control over your upcoming journey as you consider the weather you will encounter during your trip and the length of your exploration.

3. Separate your packing into small duffle bags. Have one bag for toiletries, pajamas and any medications so it comes with you every night. Have several bags with three days' worth of clothes for all passengers. Take one of these bags in with you each night as well. The two bags are a complete set to get you back on the road feeling refreshed and with fresh clothes the next day.

4. Take plenty of bags and a roll of paper towels for different purposes. A trash bag, a big laundry bag, a car sick bag, a dry goods bag for snacks and an entertainment bag will all come in handy at some point on the road. Paper towels can be used to clean up messes, as napkins to get the kids presentable, or to clean a foggy windshield. They can be used as writing paper in a pinch or to dry off after being caught in a flash rain storm. We cannot say enough about the utility of paper towels on your family road trip with kids.

5. Consider whether you will use an electronic cooler, a trucker cooking stove or a hot pot on your journey. These add to the fun and add to the options you will have while cruising down the highway. If you pack food you will eat (and can now prepare on the go), you will be saving your family time and money on the journey.

6. Pack refillable water bottles, one for each passenger, and fill up when you can. These are a great way to stay hydrated and to clean up family members that can get grungy during the trip.

7. Involve the kids in packing. Ask them which stuffed animals they would like to take and how many blankets and pillows. At some point, the kids will get homesick on your family road trip; having familiar items will make the car feel much more like home. Ask them which audio books to take on the trip, presenting them with a brief description of each of their options.

8. Consider weather and time of year when planning and packing. In warm weather, make sure to take hats and

sun screen. In colder weather, pack layers, jackets and extra blankets. If rain is likely, make sure to take a few umbrellas and ponchos.

9. You are never fully packed, so use the rest stops along your way as an opportunity to replenish your supplies and acquire any items that you forgot. If you need items of more substance like clothing or hats, a convenience store or Wal-Mart near your route will provide quick and rather inexpensive relief.

10. Put that last bag in the car, you really need to get on the road. Just go with your clothes and some goodies, and let the adventures begin!

Chapter 4

Eating on the Journey

"One cannot think well, love well, sleep well,
if one has not dined well."

— *Virginia Woolf, A Room of One's Own*

THERE ARE MANY OPTIONS for eating on the road. Prepared food can be purchased at sit down restaurants, hotels, drive thru windows, convenience stores, street fairs and rest stops. You can stop at supermarkets and purchase provisions or you can prepare food at home and bring it with you. You can choose one or more of these options each time you set out on your travels. We usually start our trips with food from home and supplement with other options as the trip progresses.

Road trip meals do not have to be relegated to sandwiches and non-perishable snacks. If you take a cooler along, you can pack perishables and you can also take leftovers from restaurants with you. If you take a trucker's oven, you can pack pre-cooked chicken fingers or hot dogs in your cooler and heat them while you drive.

We bought an inexpensive dehydrator on Amazon.com and learned to make healthy snacks like banana and apple chips. We experimented with beef jerky recipes and found one the entire family loves.

There are three basic categories of on-the-road food you can take. Perishables that need a cooler, food which can be heated in a travel oven or hot pot (usually all or part of these meals should be kept in the cooler before heating), and food that does not require refrigeration or heating.

After a lot of research and comparison shopping, we bought an Igloo Iceless 28-quart cooler. It was the right size for us because we needed a cooler that fit in the cab of our Honda Civic and we liked the price ($80 on Amazon). These 12-volt coolers come in many shapes, sizes and prices. Our favorite selling point is there is no need for cold packs to keep food fresh which means more room for food and no need to replace cold packs during the trip.

What can you put in your cooler? Anything you would put in your refrigerator. Some of our favorite cold items have been: hard boiled eggs, cheese sticks, cold cuts, yogurt tubes, cream cheese (for bagels), chicken nuggets, grilled chicken drumsticks, hot dogs, sauerkraut (if you like it on your hot dog), fresh cut fruit and vegetables, jelly, pudding pouches, milk, pasta, rice and condiments. We almost always buy apple sauce pouches and keep them in the cooler. The apple sauce would be fine unchilled, but we think it tastes better cold. We found out that some coolers double as food heaters. This feature would not be efficient for us, however, since we would need some of the food kept cool while we heat other food for our meal.

After some Googling, we discovered the RoadPro 12-volt portable oven ($36 on Amazon). This handy little gadget is used by truckers to heat their on-the-go meals and has served us well on our adventures. There are tons of positive reviews of this product online which really encouraged us to make the purchase. We just put food in a disposable loaf pan, place the pan in the oven, plug the oven into the car socket, and wait for food to heat.

What can you heat on the oven? There are many kid-friendly foods that can be prepared on the road. The grilled chicken drumsticks, chicken nuggets and hot dogs in your cooler will taste amazing when heated up in your little oven while driving at 75 miles per hour. We have never tried burgers, but they will heat up nicely in the oven as well. You can also pack cans of chili, soup and beans (they come in a can and taste better hot). You can pack these cans in your trunk, grab them when desired and heat them in your trucker's oven. Remember to take a can opener or make sure to take cans that can be opened without one.

Food that does not require refrigeration can be just as satisfying as a hot meal. We pack homemade banana muffins, homemade dried fruit, bread, rolls (for hot dogs or burgers), bagels, crescent rolls, meat sticks, beef jerky, cereal, cup of soup pouches (you will need a hot pot for these), mixed nuts, rice crispy treats, granola bars, cookies, chips, pretzels, popcorn, rice cakes, peanut butter (with jelly in the cooler), sandwich crackers, and Danny's favorite: goldfish crackers.

We take a 12-volt hot pot with us on some of our trips. We like the RoadPro 5027S 12-volt Smart Car Pot ($24 on Amazon). **Though the hot pot can be used to heat any liquid, we find that its best use is heating water** (remember those refillable water bottles you took along?). Any other liquid requires washing the pot between uses which is difficult on the road. The pot can be washed when you stop for the night at the hotel, but if all you heat up is water, the pot can be reused several times in the same day. With the hot water, we prepare cups of soup, hot chocolate, and tea. Instant coffee is also an option when you have hot water, but we still prefer stopping for coffee along the way.

With the cooler, hot pot and oven, you can prepare any meal on the road. You are only limited by your imagination and perhaps finicky eaters (we include the adults in this designation) that are sharing your adventure. We each have our favorite meal options on the road.

Danny's favorite meal is hot dogs on the go. We bring hot dog buns, sauerkraut, mustard and ketchup. Take the hot dogs and sauerkraut out of the cooler. Heat the hot dogs in the RoadPro oven and assemble. All of this can be done from the passenger seat while in motion, but can also be prepared at a picnic site.

Ben and Ella are partial to peanut butter and jelly sandwiches. These are simple to prepare, just remember to pack bread, peanut butter, jelly and something to spread with. Plastic spoons will work in a pinch, though plastic knives are ideal.

Rosa prefers a cup of soup which is quick and easy to prepare and best of all, mess free. Just heat water in the hot pot, pour mix into a paper cup with hot water and mix with a plastic spoon. Since the etiquette police are not generally traveling with us, we feel free to drink the soup right from the cup. Be careful not to overfill the hot pot with water; a sudden jerk of the car can leave you drenched or even scalded.

Car meals are fun and efficient, but we do enjoy a good meal at a nice restaurant. We found a beautiful hotel and restaurant in Baker City, Oregon called the Geiser Grand. We walked into the restored 1889 dining room and were delighted that not only could we come in for a meal without a reservation, but our casual attire was acceptable as well. In this historic location, we had an amazing meal amid beautiful architecture and outstanding atmosphere. This stop was definitely worth the slight detour.

Perhaps the most memorable sit down meal for us was not stationary at all, but rather the moving restaurant atop the Seattle Space Needle. The food was absolutely superb and, since the meal included the normally pricey tour of the top with amazing views, the price (after deducting the tour-only cost we could have incurred instead) was rather affordable. The kids enjoyed the food, but not nearly as much as they enjoyed writing notes and drawing pictures, then placing these on the wall (this is encouraged by the staff) and waiting for responses to their notes from other diners or, at a minimum, for their notes to return after the moving restaurant made a complete revolution. Seattle also makes full use of its most well-known, towering attraction by having quite a bit to see from the top on nearby buildings (among these huge spiders on one building and a smashed guitar on another).

We have a few restaurant chains that we prefer and if we find them on the road, we will try to stop at least once. Buffalo Wild Wings never disappoints. The food is consistent and the kids love the tablets they offer for entertainment. The wait staff will also generally turn TVs to the sport competitions we are most interested in watching. Perhaps most importantly, buffalo wings are a favorite food for all of us and these particular wings are always delicious.

Denny's is another of our favorite stops. A large array of foods is reasonably priced and we can always find something the kids are willing to eat. No matter what the hour, at least one of us will typically order breakfast foods. Ella is particularly partial to the claw machines usually featured in the front of the restaurant with stuffed animals to be won.

Drive-thru restaurants are an option when time is short and sometimes just because we are in the mood for something simple and familiar. Sonic has been a favorite, as have McDonald's, KFC and Taco Bell. On the road, we like to try some chain restaurants that are unfamiliar to us as well. Some of our favorite finds have been Del Taco, Godfather Pizza, Jack in the Box and In-N-Out Burger.

Convenience stores and super markets are other options for meals. You can replace the provisions you brought from home, refill your cooler, or pick up a few pre-made sandwiches or meals from the salad or hot bar. Convenience stores are especially convenient since coffee is always available and often there is a handy gas station attached for needed fuel.

There are many options for road trip eating. We find that bringing food from home is the most economical and time-saving option, but we prefer to diversify our eating experiences. If you are short on time, eat more of your meals on the go in the car with meals prepared in the car or traditional "fast food" meals that do not require a long stop if you stop at all. If you have the time, however, have a sit down meal from time to time and enjoy the local cuisine.

Getting Your Family on the Road/ Getting the Kids Involved

Here are our favorite road trip snacks. These are time-tested and the recipes have evolved to suit our tastes. The recipes are easy and fun to prepare with kids and remember that you can experiment to get your own family favorites.

HOMEMADE BEEF JERKY

Ingredients:

1 lb ground beef

1/2 cup A1 Sauce

1/4 cup Worcestershire sauce

1 tsp pepper

1 tsp garlic salt

Directions:

1. Mix all the ingredients together.

2. Place the mix on wax paper and spread with a fork until the mix is about 1/8 inch thick.

3. Cut the mix into strips and lay on to the dehydrator tray.

4. Leave on the dehydrator overnight.

5. Place strips on a cookie sheet and put in a pre-heated, 170-degree oven for 10 minutes.

6. Store in an airtight container.

BANANA CHIPS

Ingredients:

5 large bananas

1 cup lemon juice

Cinnamon

Directions:

1. Slice bananas into circles.

2. Dip slices in lemon juice.

3. Lay chips on the dehydrator tray.

4. Sprinkle with cinnamon.

5. Leave on the dehydrator overnight.

6. Store in an airtight container.

This recipe will work for apple chips as well—substitute banana slices for thinly sliced apple (best if sliced using a mandolin).

TRAVEL BANANA MUFFINS

Ingredients:

3 large ripe bananas

1 1/2 cups flour

1 teaspoon baking soda

1/2 tsp salt

3/4 cups white sugar

1 egg

1/2 cup applesauce

Directions:

1. Mix sugar, bananas, and applesauce.
2. Add dry ingredients.
3. Spray muffin tins with cooking spray.
4. Spoon batter into muffin tins.
5. Bake in a pre-heated, 350-degree oven for 25 minutes.
6. Take out of the oven, remove muffins, and let cool.
7. Store in an airtight container.

Chapter 5

Entertainment and Technology in Motion

"Are you not entertained?!"

— *Gladiator*

R OAD TRIPS ARE EXCITING. The destinations and attractions
you experience are what you, and your kids, will talk about
years after your adventures. But road trips also inherently
involve hours and hours of time in the car. As adults, we can
handle the long hours and even enjoy them. This is our time
to talk and catch up. The phone is not ringing, there are no
important meetings or conference calls to be on, and there are
no reports that need to be submitted. We do not have to worry
about housework, homework, or getting to an extracurricular

activity on time. It is just us and the road, and a chance to get reacquainted.

This is not the case for the kids. We have yet to meet a child that relishes the idea of sitting next to a sibling for eight hours and reconnecting. The only thing the kids consider connecting are their hands and feet to the other little person. We have heard many parents sigh and say "I could never be in a car for more than 6 or 8 hours with my kids." As a matter of fact, one of the main reactions people have to our road trip adventures is they cannot believe we survive these journeys "with kids."

We have to admit at first we thought to ourselves, "Wow, we must have some terrific kids." We have never considered bringing them along to be a hindrance. Actually, we feel they enhance our trips because we experience the adventure through their eyes as much as ours. Now, while we do have terrific kids, they are no different than anyone else's progeny. They complain, they whine and they fight. They have recently invented a game called "kicky wars" (the game is played just as it sounds) that we are not fond of, but they keep insisting on trying to play it in the car. On the whole, most of the time the kids are pretty great on our road trips. The secret is not really a secret at all. Bored kids will get into mischief. Occupied kids are distracted and, well, entertained.

When we started our road trips, we considered purchasing a car DVD player which comes with two screens. We thought the kids would watch movies during our travels. We figured this would keep them distracted and quiet while we drove. We priced it out and it is not that expensive, but we just could not bring ourselves to get it. The kids watch TV at home more often than we would like. This was our chance to get them away from the screen, but we still needed to give them something to pass the time.

We consulted blogs, asked questions, and researched alternatives. By our last trip, the kids had so many options for entertainment that when we offered them a chance to watch TV shows on the laptop we brought along, they got bored with it after less than half an hour. The laptop and external hard drive spent the rest of that trip in the trunk.

We have several categories of entertainment for the kids. We pack numerous audio books in the trunk and keep at least one in the car with us during the trip. We also pack reading books for the kids, notebooks for "journalizing" and drawing, activity books, crossword puzzles, Mad Libs, card and travel board games, and a tablet. We partake in more than a few family discussions in the car. We find we learn so much about the kids on these trips. In a pinch, we also offer the kids our phones so they can play some of their favorite game apps.

Audio books that we bring along are our favorite in-car entertainment. Part of the excitement building up to a trip includes choosing the stories that we will be listening to on the journey. Since we can estimate approximately how many travel hours we have, we try to pack enough listening material to last for at least three quarters of the time. We like to listen to music and talk in the car, so we do not need the audio books to cover our entire drive time. Every audio book includes a run time in its description which makes it simple to calculate the total audio book entertainment time. Some audio books have a run time of less than two hours, others have a run time of more than ten.

At first, we researched online suggestions and asked friends with kids which books they had enjoyed. At this point, we know the style and genre we like to listen to and can find suggestions for similar styles online when we run out of a particular story series that we like. The kids prefer first-person narratives, so we tend to gravitate toward that style of writing.

Rick Riordan writes some of our favorite stories. We enjoy Riordan's writing style. His main characters are young and speak in first-person, both of which appeal to the kids. His tales are exciting, clever, humorous, and tend to include very interesting historical and educational facts. His *Percy Jackson* series as well as his *Apollo* series are full of stories and facts about the Greek gods and Olympus. *The Kane Chronicles* describe the Egyptian gods and mythology while our latest discovery, *Magnus Chase*, details the Norse gods legends. After listening to the first Percy Jackson story, we picked up an anthology written by Riordan, in the voice of Percy Jackson, describing the evolution of the Greek gods. The kids loved the stories so much they started writing and acting out their own little plays based on what they learned.

We have been entertained many times (with Ben frequently playing an "extra" on "stage") on the road and back at home by their recreations. Since Ella loves babies, one of her favorite re-enactments is Demeter nursing Demophon toward immortality only to be discovered too soon. The kids both like Zeus tricking an "I love you" out of Hera while in bird-form, finally getting her to marry him. Their absolute favorite, however, is baby Hermes going on a cattle-eating spree and making innocent eyes at Apollo (owner of the eaten cattle) with a meaningful "goo goo."

From these lively, short plays, we knew Ella would excel at acting, which she has since done. She has been taking acting lessons at our local drama school and absolutely loves it. She memorizes her lines and rehearses them without us having to prod her at all. We love she has found something she excels at and enjoys. This is a particularly good thing since the multitude of sport activities we have tried to get her interested in have not panned out. We also figure memorizing all those lines is a great way to exercise her developing mind.

Another favorite children's author is Stephen Hawking. He and his daughter Lucy wrote a wonderful series about a boy named George. As George learns about the universe, and science, so does the reader. Hawking manages to describe complex scientific phenomena in a way that is not only captivating, but easy for adults and kids to truly enjoy and understand. In one part of his first book, a computer recites a nursery rhyme and then continues to analyze it scientifically. The kids still giggle when they remember that part of the book which they rewound several times to hear over and over again.

When the kids are sleeping, we have listened to Dan Brown novels. We love uncovering mysteries along with Professor Robert Langdon and learning about the art and science of symbology. The Washington Monument is mentioned in *The Lost Symbol* (Dan Brown) and *The Red Pyramid* (Rick Riordan). We all got a thrill when we finally stood in front of the monument. Does the Washington Monument hold the "last word" as Brown states in his book or is it a portal to another dimension as Riordan claims? The stories we had listened to on our trips truly enhanced that moment. That said, we are still not sure which author is correct.

A few of our other favorite audio books are *Charlie Joe Jackson* by Tommy Greenwald, *Harry Potter* by J.K. Rowling, *The Water Horse* by Dick King-Smith, *The Land of Stories* by Chris Colfer and *Running out of Time* by Margaret Peterson Haddix.

The car radio is a terrific source of entertainment as well. Besides using the CD option on the console, we love listening to the local music channels. We find certain songs we like best that are popular during the time of our trips and search all of the radio stations until those songs come on. Those songs become the soundtrack of our trips. During fantasy football season, Ben and the kids also find the local sports talk stations and get updated on their Fantasy Football players.

Both kids have their favorite authors and book styles. Danny has been reading the *Diary of a Wimpy Kid* series by Jeff Kinney and *Big Nate* books by Lincoln Peirce for years. He is also partial to the *Middle School* and *I Funny* series written by James Patterson. Ellie has discovered she enjoys books in a comic book style. She read some of Danny's *Big Nate* books (which come in comic book style as well as narrative) and has recently discovered several series she loves.

Ella loves *Phoebe and her Unicorn* adventures by Dana Simpson, *Smile* by Raina Talgemeier and *Study Hall of Justice* by Laurie King. The kids pick the books they want to take with them. Sometimes the kids will finish the books they brought for themselves and try reading the other's selections. Ellie found out that she liked the *I Funny* books and ended up reading the complete series once we got home. The kids had a few inside jokes between them as well as some great discussions after they both read the same books.

We buy new notebooks for every trip. Ellie loves to write about her feelings and experiences, and we have several notebooks full of her musings. Danny has protested many times and insists that "journalizing" will take away from his enjoyment of the trip. He wrote a list of "ten reasons why I hate journalizing" on one of our trips. That list had us roaring with laughter in the car since the reasons got sillier as Danny could not justify his distaste for writing. Eventually, we think he discarded this "top 10" list discretely in a rest stop trash can.

Danny is actually a fantastic storyteller and writes wonderful essays for school, but for some reason just does not want to write on our road trips. We do not force him. The notebooks are quite useful for playing tic-tac-toe, license plate bingo, and making lists of why you do not like to do something.

We have also taken small notebooks to Disney parks so the kids could collect autographs from the characters they came across and usually took a picture with them. The last time we stayed at a Disney hotel in Florida, we discovered we could have merchandise delivered to our room before we checked in. We ordered a small draw string bag with two bright blue autograph books in it, and a note welcoming Danny and Ellie to the park signed by Mickey himself. It was hard to keep this surprise a secret, but so much fun to walk into the room and exclaim "look kids, someone has left you both a gift."

We pack several activity books and crossword puzzles to keep the kids busy on the trip. The kids love word finds and mazes. Last year, Danny's teacher gave the class a Mad Libs book each for the summer. We took his along with us on the road. Danny and Ellie took turns filling in the silly words and cracked up reading the final stories to each other. For some reason, every time the Mad Libs story asks for a body part, the kids always choose "butt." They think this is hysterical and the specific fill-in has become another one of Danny and Ellie's little jokes. Ellie has started creating her own Mad Libs stories at home. The stories always change, but one thing stays the same: the body part fill-ins still say "butt."

The kids ran out of Mad Libs stories halfway through our first trip to California. We met our cousins in Santa Cruz for dinner that night and cousin Tina handed both kids gift bags that contained adorable stuffed animals and, most importantly, fresh Mad Libs. This was fantastic and a total surprise. The kids enjoyed the stories all the way home and we have made sure to pack new Mad Libs on every trip since.

The kids love playing Monopoly and The Game of Life at home. They brought Monopoly on one of our shorter road trips, but playing the full-size game was difficult in the back seat of a moving car. Luckily, game maker Hasbro produces miniature versions of these games for travel. We bought mini Monopoly and mini Clue online, and found a card version of The Game of Life. The kids enjoyed playing the board games, but ended up losing most of the little pieces in the car, so they did not get to play the games many times.

———

The Game of Life card game was great for the trip. The kids got many hours of play without destroying the game—much. Some of the cards did get bent, but on the whole the game made it home intact. **We have decided to forgo the board games on future adventures and stick to card games which take up less room in the car and do not have so many small pieces that can be lost.** We might consider bringing mini board games along again when the kids are older and more careful (we can hope anyway). These games could all be played at hotel stops or during picnic lunches on the road, but are not such a great idea for a moving vehicle.

We pack a tablet on our trips. It is a simple Kindle Fire without many bells and whistles, but it has all the features that we need. We started taking it along because we loaded it with fun eBooks for the kids. It was also great because it has a camera which gave us an additional option for taking pictures and posting them to Facebook.

The kids have a few game apps that they love playing on the tablet, so that gives them something to do in the car as well. One of the features that has become a handy entertainment option: the NetFlix app that we loaded onto the tablet. We have found some motels do not have programming the children like. Also, there are mornings where we would like to sleep in and recharge a little more than the kids. During those times, we prefer they do not watch morning TV which will wake us up.

For both reasons, NetFlix on the tablet has been the solution. The kids can watch their favorite shows from home on the tablet and keep the volume low enough so that we can get extra sleep.

We make sure to connect the tablet and our phones to the hotel Wi-Fi before we go to sleep. The next morning, the kids will keep themselves entertained with the electronics until we are ready to get up and while we start to get ready for a new day of travel.

The latest electronic entertainment solution we have come up with involves two pieces of technology. The first is a 2 tera-byte external USB hard drive and the second is a simple lap-top computer. We have loaded the external drive with several kid-friendly TV shows and movies. The tablet and phones will stream TV shows and movies when Wi-Fi is available, but the laptop is great for times were there is no Wi-Fi or a finicky sig-nal. We would have to pack hundreds of DVDs in the car to have the same amount of entertainment packed into our little, exter-nal hard drive—it is a great space saver.

The best electronic tool we take on the road with us is our mobile smart phone. We use it as a GPS, using Siri and Waze as primary applications. Siri is the proprietary Apple assistant and can do much more than act as a GPS. The kids love asking her random trivia questions to see what she brings back. There are also a few especially entertaining questions to which she has several prepared responses. Some of our favorites are "Siri, what does the fox say," "Siri, what is 0 divided by 0," and "I love you, Siri." Go ahead, give these a try yourself.

Waze is a social media GPS app. Users of the app will update it with traffic patterns, accidents, and police presence. Waze will also suggest several dining options on the road. We have used both Siri and Waze on all our trips. We have even used Waze in-ternationally on a trip to Canada and it has yet to steer us wrong.

The phone is also a great resource for on-the-road research. If we are running ahead of schedule or just want to make a change to our travel plans, we can search Google on the spot and find great options and alternatives at our finger tips.

The smart phones are also our travel cameras. The resolutions on today's smart phones are superior to the digital cameras we had only a few years ago. The kids use the phones to play games and watch TV shows when we are on the road. Our travels would look very different without our little smart devices.

In addition to our car chargers, we make sure to carry portable chargers with us. We have found ourselves away from our car or an outlet for an extended period on a few occasions. Having a small energy port at our disposal has been invaluable. Losing power in our phones does not only mean that Grandma cannot get ahold of us until we recharge, it also could mean a lost photo opportunity and we just cannot have that.

We enjoy talking to each other on the road because we lead such hectic lives during the year. The kids have their extracurricular activities during the week and on the weekends. We both have full-time jobs and tend to get home relatively late. We rarely get a chance to just sit, relax and talk. Our car rides give us this precious time.

The kids tell us about their friends and things that are happening in school. We discover new things about them every time we go on a road trip. One of our favorite discussions starts with a recap of our favorite activities of the day. At the end of the trip, we like to discuss our favorite activity, favorite stop, or the trip in its entirety. This not only gives us an idea of what we would like to do on future trips, but also allows us to learn more about each other and sometimes ourselves.

Getting Your Family on the Road/ Getting the Kids Involved

1. Before you get on the road, have a variety of entertainment options planned and packed. The experience of sitting for many hours in close quarters with your family can be wonderful, but you want to hedge your bets by bringing along different types of entertainment. Bring plenty.

2. Have the children take the books they are reading from home (and perhaps a few past favorites), discuss which audio books you want to hear as a family, and bring along some games (without little pieces).

3. As you enjoy hours of audio books, pay attention to the themes and the authors you are enjoying the most. Many of these authors have written other, similar books and there will be many other books similar in subject matter and target audience.

4. Notebooks are handy for journaling, but can also be used for kid-generated crossword puzzles, hangman games, tic-tac-toe, or drawing the latest attraction (remember to bring a few crayons).

5. There are so many multimedia options at home, bring some of the portable ones along. You will have your

phones as a necessity, but bring along a tablet or Nintendo DS as well. If you have the room, a laptop with a packed external hard drive can come in handy.

6. Phones, with great resolution, are a wonderful option for picture-taking during your trip. Smart phones also come with handy apps for travel and have other apps that will appeal to the kids while cruising down the highway.

7. Given how many uses you will have for your phones, bring all the car and electrical outlet chargers you need (pack at least one backup cord). Take some portable chargers along as well.

8. At the motel or hotel, connect phones and tablets to Wi-Fi to give the kids options besides the TV which may not have anything of interest to them. This can be a great strategy for giving the adults a little more rest time in the morning.

9. Remember to use the many hours you will have in the car to engage in conversations with your kids and with each other. There is usually not too much uninterrupted discussion time at home so this is an amazing opportunity to get to know each other better.

10. Pick up some notebooks, electronic devices, Mad Libs, audio books and games, you really need to get on the road. With your entertainment options packed, let your adventures begin!

Chapter 6

Stumbles on Your Trip

"Failures, repeated failures, are finger posts on the road to achievement. One fails forward toward success."

— C. S. Lewis

As you head off into the wilds of the American wide open spaces, well-armed with the best planned route ever woven together with exciting well-researched destinations and a car packed with every necessity, remember, things will still go wrong. Our family has encountered a plethora of disasters on the road and learned quite a bit from each one. We try to learn from our mishaps and try harder to avoid repeating them.

We are not going to promise you will not have some hiccups and missteps on your road journey with kids. But, you might not run into the exact situations we have encountered on our trips. So what advice can we give you? Plenty.

Some road trip disasters are avoidable and others you will just need to ride out. You can avoid running out of gas in the middle of somewhere Colorado at the end of December if you start looking for a gas station when the gas gauge inches below half a tank. If you get stuck in traffic for hours, however, you might still end up with the gas light on, holding your breath and praying for just a few more miles so you can make it to that next open gas station.

You can avoid bad weather by keeping up with the weather reports. But, you might not be able to avoid sliding into a snow bank on an icy road if there are no snow chains to be purchased for miles. That is, unless you prepare ahead of time and purchase those tire chains in advance.

You will fight on the road. This is unavoidable. **Any family, no matter how well adjusted, will have a few misunderstandings and tiffs on the road.** You will be tired, dirty and cranky, and, having spent hours in close quarters, you will end up locking horns. Sleep deprivation is one of our nemeses. We can manage most situations, but if both adults are tired we will fight over the smallest differences of opinion and sometimes more serious matters. Unfortunately, since we prefer to road trip to the extreme, sleep deprivation will happen.

The testiest we have ever been, not just on a trip but ever, was outside of the Grand Canyon. Quick tip for the Grand Canyon: without prior reservations at the fairly pricey Grand Canyon hotels, you will not stay closer than 90 minutes from the Canyon entrance in Flagstaff if you are visiting from the South Rim. There are no hotels, motels, or campsites between Flagstaff and the Grand Canyon. We knew this when we headed to the Canyon late at night at the end of a long day. What we did not know is at the end of December, in the middle of a storm that was sweeping the Midwest, Flagstaff hotels and motels would be booked solid.

We explored the Canyon in the dead of night, visibility was not great, and ice and snow were on the road. As we made our way back down the dark road that led back to Flagstaff, we started trying to book a room for the night. There were no rooms available unless you count the one literally flee-bitten motel that had one room left. Every review of this motel said it was dirty and riddled with bed bugs. Thankfully, the only available room had a broken lock and the door was stuck so the receptionist had to refund our payment.

There were no rooms available in the next three towns toward Nevada. We were tired and this was 1 a.m. when we realized we could not get a hotel, motel or campsite other than our "car hotel." There was, shall we say, a difference of opinion and to be honest, we still have not quite resolved who was "right." In the interest of harmony, we will not elaborate on that point.

Ben thought "I will stay up while the rest of you sleep and drive around the Grand Canyon" and in the back of his mind also thought "We can get into the Park for free overnight (the gate is open, but unstaffed according to the internet)." Rosa thought a little differently. Hanging around in Grand Canyon National Park overnight seemed dangerous and foolish, the perfect set-up for a cautionary-tale local news story the next day. Sleep deprived, after a long day of traveling, all Mom could think was that she had to protect her two little kids sleeping soundly in the back seat. What if we ended up sleeping in the park when some stranger decided to break our car windows? There must be a room to sleep in, however long a drive that would be.

The kids voted (both in deep sleep) to keep sleeping in the back seat which was a successful vote for a while. Ben was still intent on traveling the hour and a half back to the Canyon. Around 3 a.m., Mom and Dad were arguing and there were some unkind words, even a few scattered, sleep-deprivation-fueled threats. Let us just say one of us left the car and the other considered, however briefly, driving off with one fewer passenger.

So get some sleep and plan for getting stuck without a room. Whether you are going to sleep in the car or push on to a motel or campsite, have a basic plan and remember probably the most important rule of the road: **you have to finish this trip together, so at some point in disagreements, find some middle ground and move on.** For us, it meant not seeing the Grand Canyon on this entire trip. We were all too shell-shocked by the fighting to even consider a stop there on our return journey.

The most avoidable disaster of our travels (nearly) happened on Christmas day in Colorado and, actually, disaster was avoided. But the near-miss made a mark in our memories as deep as if we had been stuck in a small Colorado town for about two days longer than intended. It is easy enough to find gas stations along your route, but it turns out the southwest United States has the fewest gas stations per square mile than anywhere else in the nation. Even as we learned that, we still got stuck about four times on the same trip with a gas range of 10 miles or less.

But on Christmas day, we were at "Gas Range 0" with no gas station in sight. Siri failed us because though she took us to the closest gas station, this particular one had a nice note on the door: these fine folks would not be opening back up until December 27 at 9 a.m. Four blocks away, we decided the safest option was to pull into an open, local diner and wait out AAA's road service for however long that would take.

We opened our Waze GPS travel app just on a whim: 3 miles to another gas station. Would it be open (remember, "Gas Range 0" and we had a nice, warm, open diner right in front of us)? We made the attempt and found the Waze-recommended gas station with a few customers inside the small convenience store and gas pumps open for business. Whew, we could breathe again!

Two road trips later on the same route with the gas light on, we had the option of going forward and taking a chance on finding a gas station or going backward 20 miles to a gas station that Waze was sure about. We spent the extra 50 minutes it took to go with certainty; we had learned our lesson. That was a good move, it turned out, because when we continued our venture forward it was well beyond our initial "range" to get a working gas station in the dead of night. It is best to avoid the same mistake twice, after all.

The first time Rosa travelled through Colorado, years before kids and before she even met Ben, she was driving home from California from her internship in Los Angeles. She and her roommate entered the Centennial State and thoroughly enjoyed a wonderful visit to Mesa Verde. After a lovely night in a small, very pink motel, they headed east again towards New Jersey and home.

A rock slide blocked the pass that led home and they ended up driving for miles on a very dark road praying the signs that said "Beware of Elk" were friendly warnings of something that does not happen very often. Rosa still remembers half expecting a ghost hitchhiker to appear strolling on the side of that pitch black highway. They were tired, hungry, and desperate to find a ladies' room. They drove for hours, with no town or motel in sight. When they finally found a town, all motels were booked.

They finally found one available room at a Howard Johnson hotel. Back then they still had smoking rooms and one of those was the only room available. It reeked of cigarettes and they did not care. Rosa still gets a warm and fuzzy feeling every time she sees a Howard Johnson. To this day, she remembers this evening as her best night's sleep ever.

Years later, we drove as a family into Colorado with the intention of spending the night in a Holiday Inn Express just outside of Mesa Verde. An hour away from that wonderful hotel, hot tub, swimming pool and soft, clean beds, we hit a small snag. The same pass that had a rock slide all those years ago was now blocked by an avalanche.

We detoured and ended up inside a National Forest where we found a few hikers walking in the snow. They told us to "hunker down" at the nearest town and wait out the storm. We would not give up, though, and drove for three hours using a different road only to find another roadblock at yet another unsafe Colorado road. We drove through a terrifying snow drift that left us surrounded by stark, white nothingness.

Ben stopped several times on the highway unable to continue with zero visibility. We eventually had a quick family meeting on the road and decided to reroute our trip entirely and go south to New Mexico. **No matter how risk tolerant you may be, when you are taking a road trip with your kids, your family's safety is your top concern.** Be flexible enough to reroute if needed.

The night we completely rerouted our trip to New Mexico, trying to escape the snow and ice of Colorado, we headed for Roswell. A quick note about Roswell: if you have heard of it from the TV show named after it, or you are a fan of the *X-Files*, or "lunatic" UFO theories, you should know the residents embrace all things "alien."

The journey to Roswell was difficult with a few spots of snow drifts that made for zero visibility. So much so that in uncharacteristic fashion for us, we literally stopped at several points on highways for the snow winds to die down at least a bit. As we continued our drive south to Roswell, however, the snow totally cleared up with only a snow dusting on the roads. What a relief. There we were at 2 a.m. local time (even worse, our biological clocks still said 4 a.m. New Jersey time). Of course, we had to take a number of selfies with a human-sized, green alien right outside the Super 8 motel lobby. This cheered up the adults though the kids were long sleeping.

A quick note about time zones. The "lower 48" United States is split into four time zones. From the east coast to the west coast, in order, are the Eastern, Central, Mountain, and Pacific time zones. Each time you cross a time zone, you gain or lose an hour, depending on your direction. East to west, gain an hour.

West to east, lose one. This time travel needs to be considered when traveling to a destination across time zones.

If you are going west and crossing a time zone, you have an additional hour to get to it. If you are traveling east, remember you actually have one hour less. So, if a destination is four hours away "as the crow flies" you have five hours to get there going west, but three hours to get there going east. Look at a time zone map and be aware of the states to which you will be time jumping. It is fun on the road to pass signs that announce time zone changes. We enjoy these almost as much as we enjoy "Welcome to" state signs.

In Roswell, we walked into the motel lobby and the receptionist said pretty poignantly (at 2 a.m., this actually seemed a bit accusatory): "You know, we are expecting 24 inches of snow tomorrow." It did not seem quite real with not more than a hint of snow on the ground we had just walked from the car. All we could manage was: "Are you sure?" "Yes, the news says over 20 inches starting tomorrow around noon." This was pretty easy to confirm on Weather.com, it turned out, which we did once we got into our room.

Since we are alien enthusiasts, especially Ben, a plan quickly emerged: see the UFO museum the minute it opened the next day (a few minutes before 9 a.m., we were pacing back and forth in front of the entrance) and gun it outta Dodge, well, outta Roswell anyway. We did and it was a great museum for the UFO conspiracy theorist, or even the UFO conspiracy theorist fan. We still caught a slippery form of snow right around Albuquerque, but emerged unscathed and continued our journey. The few hours difference in leaving Roswell, we are sure, made a huge difference in getting past the worst of the snowfall.

When considering weather, time of year and region will be more of a consideration than the exact locations you are headed. If you are going in summer, weather is going to be less of a factor, but be especially careful in winter. Weather.com, powered by the Weather Channel, gives you an easy-to-read 10 day forecast and you want to be on the lookout for snow.

Rain will rarely pull you off the road, but snow in certain amounts especially with significant wind will stop you every time. In Colorado, use local phone advisory numbers and web-sites to make sure the "passes" are open. If you are in the Colorado region and are braving potentially closed "passes" then bring a 4-wheel drive vehicle, tire chains, or better yet, detour away from the state.

Remember *The Shining* took place in Colorado and, if you are stuck in the kind of weather featured in the movie, you may be closer than you think to a Jack Nicholson moment on a road trip with your kids. If it is the American southwest, do not bother thinking "south = warmer" the way we do on the east coast. This is snow country.

On another leg of this trip in the region, we tried to get to Mesa Verde and got there in the dark. We drove up the mountain, hoping to find beautiful views and possibly see a few cliff dwellings in the twinkle of overhead flood lights. Unfortunately, you cannot see anything at Mesa Verde at night. Snow and ice make the trip treacherous and very dangerous. It turns out you are legally required to have snow chains on your tires in these weather conditions. This is a fact we learned only once we got down the mountain safely after finding all the roads to the ruins closed. Disappointed, we had to keep going and decided to drive to Denver from there.

It was New Year's Eve and we hoped to enjoy some Denver fireworks. The trip was long and difficult and took us thorough a winding, mountainous road. We were on the road when the clock struck midnight, far away from any town featuring fireworks that evening. We have a great family selfie taken on New Year's Eve in the car, somewhere on the Colorado mountains. **Remember to keep your kids in a festive mood despite any adversity you are facing and any anxiety you may be feeling; they will take their cues from you.**

We made it to Denver in the early hours of the morning, found a hotel and had a very good night's sleep. We did get back to Colorado on a trip later that year and we did see Mesa Verde; travel enough and time will eventually be on your side.

You might be on the road for a while and find yourself far from home base when disaster strikes; not where you are, but back home. We were having a wonderful time at Universal Studios, Florida. Ben was invited to dance with minions from *Despicable Me* during a street performance and later got a chance to have a cockatoo land on his arm during an animal actor performance. While we were standing in line for the *Men in Black* ride, we got a call from Rosa's mother (she was in charge of picking up the mail, checking on the house and feeding the kids' fish while we were away). She was wondering where our mailbox was.

It turned out that on the day we left someone had taken our mailbox off the post. Our mail carrier was kind enough to leave our mail on the porch, but the mailbox was gone. We called the postmaster from the road and he told us we could stop our mail delivery until we got a new box, but they would continue to deliver to our porch if we would prefer (we preferred the latter option). A friend of Rosa's mother installed a new mailbox for us the next day and the problem was solved.

A few days later disaster struck again. A text from Rosa's mother told us both betta fish the kids had managed to keep alive for months had expired on the same day. We considered telling the kids this terrible news once we got back home, but then decided to tell them sooner in order to start the healing process. Tears flowed and loving memories were shared. Ella said it best: "He was a great fish, we bonded."

We had a family vote and decided to get a hamster when we got home. The kids' spirits bounced right back after that. Hammy Fuzzball (her name was chosen after another family vote) would join our family as soon as we got back.

Disasters will happen at home while you are on the road. There might be events that will require you to shorten your trip. Other disasters back home can be dealt with from the road or when you get back. Evaluate the problem and deal with it as needed.

There is one minor "disaster" to consider, though the word may be overstating it: missing an attraction on the route because of timing. **We tend to think of travel with 24 hours in the day,**

but attractions are not always open. We missed "Four Corners National Monument" twice in the same trip because we got there an hour or two after closing. We will get to Four Corners someday, but the stop has eluded us four times thus far (one miss for each corner, we suppose).

It is not hard to live with in retrospect, but in the moment there can be some regret. **If a particular stop is important to you, go to the website, figure out the timing and leave a good 2 hour buffer to get there.** If a site closes at 6:30 p.m., it does you no good to get there at 7 p.m., but it is no better to get there at 6:25 p.m. Generally, your visit is not as important to the staff (albeit staff in the tourism industry) as it is to you.

A perfect example of this: we arrived at the Grand Canyon West Rim with a half-hour to spare before closing and all the tours were full. We tried to pull the New Jersey card ("I guess we will have to go back to New Jersey and miss this") and it just did not work. The response we remember from a lovely cashier was something along the lines of "I guess so."

You may as well have a safe word or "let's stop this" hand gesture agreed upon in advance once fighting starts. There is nothing worse than fighting on the road because, in a cramped car, you cannot exactly close the door to not upset the little ones. They are right in it with you. Get some sleep; **there is not an attraction anywhere in the nation that is worth a fight you will absolutely regret and will not be able to forget when you get back to life at home**. As a family, there is no night of good sleep—even 4 blessed hours—that we have regretted in our journeys.

It is especially important the kids get enough sleep. So take at least two pillows per kid (adults can borrow these pillows too in times of need). **Make sure they take stuffed animals from home, the ones they have named.** For us, we take "Nana" for Danny and "Pookie" for Ella. "Nana" is time-beaten and "Pookie" is pretty new in comparison, but they both enjoy our journeys right along with us. A blanket or two for each kid also comes in handy; these **blankets are much easier to wash once we return home than the car itself!** Truth be told, we have given up on a clean car so clean-ish will have to do.

The rule of thumb on gas: **if you are at less than 40% of your full gas tank and not on major highways, fill up.** This is a great chance to stretch your legs, get a few inexpensive snacks, meet a local or two (while avoiding political discussions), use the restroom with the kids and get some caffeine. Gas up often, just as you should change your oil often at home in preparation for long road trips. Your car is saving you plenty of money on vacation, treat her well.

We do not have any particularly sage advice about wild animals crossing the road. We have heard horror stories from others, though, and a collision can end a trip or at least your excitement for that trip. Enjoy nature's beautiful creatures and try to avoid vehicular contact whenever possible.

We have seen some gorgeous creatures: wild horses in Assateague; a moose, several buffalo and deer in Yellowstone; a coyote on Mulholland Drive in Los Angeles; prairie dogs in Arizona; eagles in flight in Wabasha, Minnesota and many other exceptional creatures. Take a picture or two when you can and slow down whenever possible. We have stared down deer at night in many states including Colorado, Utah and Arizona with a telepathic plea: let's not make this a night to remember! It has worked for us. No harm in you giving it a try, but when you find wildlife on your journeys, slow down or even stop your car just in case.

Getting Your Family on the Road/ Getting the Kids Involved

1. Take sleep into account when planning your route. In our 20s, we could still pull all-nighters and function the next day. Now, somewhat past those days of our carefree youth, sleep is not something we can go without for too long. We have no problem settling for 5 hours of sleep, even 4 can suffice some of the time. Lack of any sleep, however,will only lead to the risk of falling asleep at the wheel. With sleep deprivation, every kind of disaster, even a minor setback, will seem insurmountable.

2. Our top tip to avoid disaster: get some sleep, all of you. The kids will likely be lulled to sleep by the motion of the car; we do not know of any better sleep that the kids get than on the road. But adults, you will need a daily bed of some kind.

3. Fight the urge to fight. Let's face it, you did not choose the kids, but you did choose your partner and you are in this together. When one of the kids asks us who our favorite is, we always dodge that question and say each other (not even close, kids). A road trip is the perfect time to model

life partnership for the little ones. So, try not to sweat the small stuff. There will be journeys ahead to see the great site that is now closed, to travel the path that is now snow-covered, or to see the view that you had your heart set on. What is sure is you want to reach home again on speaking terms and better yet, excited for the next trip.

4. Of all that happens on your road trip with your kids, fights have a way of being the most memorable. Move on, there are great sites to see and adventures to be had.

5. Gas up often, especially when you are off of the major highways of your trip. We adults have different "rules" for when to gas up, but we both agree that running out of gas is the surest way to get your timing off and your anxiety on. Look for signs that take you directly to gas stations. Sometimes these are off the beaten path, however, so whenever possible go to the gas stations you can see from the road. That is the surest way to lose little time and get the fuel that makes a family road trip possible in the first place.

6. You are going to have to weather the weather, so make good choices. The first good choice is avoiding snow at the earliest stages of planning. If the weather in the part of the country you are planning to travel is wretched, or even can be horrible, explore a different region this time around. In summer, you usually have a "weather freebie" so plan your summer trips to areas that are more risky in the colder months. On the road, detour if necessary.

7. Even with a great plan for a trip you are in the middle of taking, you can re-plan the trip if you hit a snowy wall (we

have). Go to TripAdvisor on your phone (preferably the passenger, of course), consult Google and plan a new route that avoids snow drifts, ice patches and zero visibility. It is worth it. Remember you are your own travel agent and tour guide. It is okay if you miss a planned attraction. You can always go back another time. Sometimes the places you find on your detours are even the most memorable experiences of the trip.

8. Turn the animal problem upside down. Hitting an animal is the quickest way to end a trip and kill your enthusiasm (among other things). But kids generally love animals so go with that. Have the kids research which animals live in the part of the country you are exploring. At National Parks, take the brochure and have the kids study which animals they should be on the lookout for.

9. Have the kids take pictures of new and interesting animals along the way. If the kids like to draw, have them sketch out the animals in their notebooks. If the animals are far enough from the car, you can even venture out and take a picture with that wild buffalo. We are talking really far away, though; no feeding, no petting and no adopting the wild. And brake for animals any chance you get.

10. Put away any lingering doubts and take a deep breath, you really need to get on the road. Just go, know the odds are in your favor (especially with good planning), and let the adventure begin!

Chapter 7

Building Your Family Legend

"Carpe Diem. Seize the Day... Make Your Lives Extraordinary."

—*Dead Poets Society*

PLANNING THE ROAD TRIP is almost as exciting as the trip itself. We update each other and discuss ideas. We share our plans with friends, family and colleagues. "We are going to Alaska this summer." "We are driving to California this winter break." "We are taking the kids to Disney for the weekend." These declarations and more have been made often enough that people often ask us, "So, where are you going next?" and we most likely already have a plan in mind, ready to share.

While we are on the road trip, we Tweet, post on Facebook and text updates as we explore and discover the country. When we return, we share our adventures. Sharing and retelling our stories gives us a chance to experience our adventures again, so we never shy away from a chance to answer the question "How was your trip?" in vivid detail.

One of our favorite trip stories was nowhere near the longest trip, but by far the most constrained. Rosa decided we should go to Ohio over a long weekend. At this point we had not visited the state and it seemed like a good time to add another pin to our map. A co-worker mentioned the Football Hall of Fame is in Ohio and Rosa researched and discovered it is in Canton.

The Saturday we were planning to go, Ben and Danny had an in-person Fantasy Football draft in the evening and the following Monday was the Labor Day holiday. We needed to be back by Monday night for school and work the next day. "Ohio" was this trip's battle cry and the (field) goal: the Football Hall of Fame.

What made this trip "legendary" mostly was the narrative: starting by drafting the boys' 2014 season Fantasy team, traveling to the biggest museum in the world devoted to football and coming back in one piece to start the school year the next day. The guys had ratcheted up their excitement at the Fantasy draft and that got all of our adrenaline pumping.

Ben and Danny came home from the draft and we headed out the door. This was a time where we still pre-booked hotel rooms and we arrived at the Holiday Inn Express in Pittsburg in the wee hours of Sunday morning. Ben had done some research of his own and found a wonderful aviary, the National Aviary, which we visited on Sunday morning. We were pleased to discover that close by street parking was free for the holiday weekend. We spent the morning exploring the aviary, watching live bird shows and having a wonderful time as a large array of small birds zipped past our heads. Then we headed to Canton.

The museum was excellent with assorted memorabilia and, best of all, the Super Bowl experience which is a multimedia immersion where we got to relive the most exciting moments of Manning-Wilson where the Seahawks (at that time, our stealth favorite) came away on top. Rosa took a great picture where Ben picked up both kids to make a human field goal, with a giant football behind them right in the middle. That picture was worth 3 points on that road trip, for sure.

On our longest trip, "Alaska," we did have the most memorable, legendary experience. It started with a question to our Alaskan Airlines stewardess—could we have airplane wings for the kids? What came back were two metal airline wings, the real thing instead of what we had assumed would be plastic. We had two kid co-pilots now sitting with the grownups in coach.

Landing in Juneau, however, we got a fantastic offer. Danny was invited to take a personal tour of the cockpit and get his picture taken with the pilot. We had just left the airplane and the stewardess explained that we could not go back, but they wanted to make an exception for Danny. She offered to take Rosa's phone and take pictures for us. When she came back there were pictures of Danny sitting in the pilot's chair with the pilot right beside him. What a wonderful experience for our little boy and we had some amazing pictures to remember it by. Of course, one of those pictures ended up on Twitter and Facebook. Two quick lessons: **always ask for and always say yes to legend-building paraphernalia and experiences**.

Disneyland provided another legendary experience as seen through the joy and excitement of the kids. Their favorite ride was "Autopia" by Honda, a car-driving experience with a tracked loop, where they got to drive their parents around for a change. Danny kept saying "Daddy gave me a real driving lesson—when can I get a real license?" which was adorable. Little Ella showed her aggressive side by holding tightly to the wheel and shouting, "Let's see what this puppy can do," leaving Rosa in stitches. Both kids loved having the chance to be in the driver's seat, after being driven all over the country by Mom and Dad.

One of Rosa's favorite stories was an unplanned detour on our way to Yellowstone National Park. We were having a lovely breakfast in Cody, Wyoming just outside the Park and Ben decided that we should go horseback riding. There is something exquisite about the mountains in Wyoming that is difficult to capture in words. We found a small ranch right outside a museum that offered horseback rides in the valley. The four of us got on our respective horses. This was the first time either of the kids sat on a real horse.

They had ridden ponies before, but this was a new and exciting experience for them. We rode into the valley, surrounded by mountains, and watched an eagle circle lazily above us. We rode by a turquoise river that glittered in the sun. The air was crisp and clean and the horses were extremely well trained and well-mannered.

We had a wonderful time and headed for Yellowstone a few hours later than planned. It is important to note here that poor Ellie was saddle sore for days after this experience, so this is a possible downside that should be considered before attempting to go on a long horseback riding experience with your kids. She has asked to go riding again since that trip, even later that same trip, so we will try it again on one of our next adventures. Every time she recalls this first experience, however, either she or Mom mutters the lament "saddle sore."

We remember these moments because they were exceptional, but we remember many more moments and have a daily chronicle of our trips through social media. We also have taken to journaling as parents and have encouraged the kids to "journalize" along with us. For the adults, the adventures we had before we were 10 years old are pretty much lost on us. There are some adorable pictures, some of them even have some context (usually a year or an age) written on the back (remember when photographs were developed on paper?). For our kids, having the adventures of their thus far short lifetimes, we want more to look back on as we build out our family legend.

Journaling is great. We type up notes when we get back home and store these on our hard drives (backups are a great idea, but since we do not partake of that custom we are a "blue screen of death" away from losing some of these pieces). Recapping is also a great way to remember that attraction you just visited on the road. We ask the kids after each stop: "So what was your favorite part?" That question is a nice primer for their journaling, but also signals to you what they are finding most memorable about your adventures.

These salient memories can inform your future choices. For a long time, Danny's favorite attraction of our travels was

Medieval Times. We caught the show in Maryland and Danny loved the pageantry and action. One of his favorite parts which we would not have thought of, turns out, was being given full permission to eat with his hands since Medieval Times does not offer silverwear.

When we later travelled to Las Vegas, we had time for one show and knew Danny would have a favorite: a similar show at the Excalibur Hotel, holiday themed at the end of December. It was a hit with all of us, especially with our little guy. Lesson learned: **favorite attractions create opportunities for statistical success in the future**; it felt like we had beaten the house in Vegas.

Cameras are great, both for you and the kids. We have tried several approaches. The first was giving the kids disposable cameras. The cameras themselves are relatively inexpensive, but developing the pictures costs more than purchasing a low-end digital camera. If you want to repeat the disposable camera experience, there is also the additional cost for the next trip. However, since the disposable camera is not very expensive, losing or breaking one will not be too upsetting.

We almost lost a disposable camera once. We were at Mount Rushmore, leaning against one of the guard rails. Danny had taken a few pictures of the monument and was very proud of his photography skills. The camera slipped out of his pocket and landed behind the railing. Rosa sighed and said, "oh well, it was a cheap camera anyway." Danny was devastated. The camera was cheap, but his pictures were on it and they were irreplaceable.

Ben leapt over the railing (do not try that trick yourself, we are pretty sure he was not supposed to do that). He retrieved the camera and jumped back in front of his adoring, grateful son. This instantly became a great, legendary story. The kids still talk about that moment where Daddy heroically saved the day.

If you do not want to go the disposable camera route, there are other options. There are very inexpensive digital cameras with low resolution. The kids get to see the pictures they take on a small viewing window in the back of the camera and they can delete pictures they do not like. You can lend them your smart phone which most likely has better resolution and has the ability to upload pictures immediately to social media. **Social media is the best way to chronicle memories; it gives us a date and time where we recently took a picture, gives the picture context and gives us a specific location to frame the memory.** Social media is a great set of tools, an extension of memory for all of us. We have picked up a few tips to share.

Facebook is, for us, still the most versatile of social media tools. The kids do not have accounts, but Mom and Dad usually "tag" each other so our friends can enjoy our latest stop and musings. **We "check in" at locations now which is a great way to show other visitors what we liked, a fantastic way for our friends to find out more about the attraction itself, and a nice way for us to go back years later and remember what state a certain attraction was actually in.** Facebook does not limit our characters and in some sense is more protected from the searchable, always-on, internet world.

One of Rosa's favorite posts is a picture of a spontaneous stop we made to see the biggest ball of twine in Minnesota. We had the time to take a short detour from our planned route and found out the attraction was just a short drive out of our way. As we researched the attraction, we discovered that Weird Al had written a song about this very same Ball of Twine and a family that decided to go to see it. We posted our picture next to the ball and added a link to the song; that was a great post.

Twitter is our second choice for family and friends, but our first choice for cyber interaction. Twitter blends the personal and the corporate, so that we can pick up unknown fan "followers" or we can get some much-enjoyed corporate attention. The 140-character limit is usually not terrible since Twitter is pretty forgiving of shortened words or half-thoughts. A picture within each post is a must for the traveling family with kids.

In our own "Hall of Fame" are travel interactions with @Honda, @AlaskaAir [Alaska Airlines], @GoParks [National Park Foundation] and @MountRushmoreNM [Mount Rushmore National Memorial]. **Use the #hashtags, use the corporate handles.** Let these folks know you want to speak with them, it puts the "social" into the media and answers back will always put a smile on your face.

A new addition to our social media platform favorites is Instagram. We like to doctor the pictures to make them burst off of the screen while retaining the basic content and storyline. We experiment with lighting, color and a host of other features to make our cellular phone pictures look more artistic and unique. The best part of Instagram is attracting other users with a variety of #hashtags that will garner the attention of like-minded users with these hashtagged interests. Of course, we enjoy a good "like" but a "follow" is a bigger compliment on the platform. Instagram allows you to attract unknown fan followers like Twitter, but the pictures themselves are broadcast further than on Twitter because of the prolific use of the hashtags and the lack of the 140-character limit.

Our family likes to have fun, even on the internet, during our travels. Why does it matter and why should you join in the enjoyment? No matter how many trips you take, you want to cherish them. Part of your return on investment calculation has to include how memorable these trips will be. There is no doubt that much of the value is in the trip experience itself. A few moments will live on in your memory bank even with no technology at all. But you want more than that. Your kids are growing up quickly, too quickly, and your adventures with them are limited. Make the most of these travels and use the best tools to easily chronicle your journeys.

In honor of making the most of it, parents, plan some surprises along the way. Our best surprise was in taking the kids for the first time to Disneyworld. We did not tell them where we were going intentionally, we did not even divulge the state name until we stopped at the Welcome Center in Florida. We arrived about 10 miles out and asked Ella to look out the window at the sign. "What do you see?" "It says Exit." That answer took us off track into laughing for a few moments, but we parents pressed on. "Look at that other sign." "It says DISNEY!" A few miles out, like Super Bowl MVPs, we announced to the kids "We're going to Disneyworld!"

Not all surprises are for kids. The official start to our 49-state challenge was a trip northward to Maine which was in essence a trip to Vermont with a quick dip into Maine for a delicious lobster dinner. For this trip we booked two hotel nights in advance (though we have changed our pre-booking ways since then). The first night would be at a picturesque hotel in New Hampshire and the second at a family-run dairy farm in Vermont. Once the hotels were booked, Rosa researched the area and found out that among many other wonderful attractions, Vermont is home to Ben & Jerry's Ice Cream. This weekend happened to coincide with Ben's birthday and Rosa decided to surprise him.

She called Ben & Jerry's and told the very friendly customer service representative the day they planned to visit was Ben's birthday. The representative told her that, upon request, they would put up a banner with a birthday wish for Ben, give him a free birthday cone, and have a "Happy Birthday" pin ready for him at the door. Rosa made the arrangements and bought him an ice cream cake as well.

When Ben walked into the main entrance, he still had no idea that Rosa had put this plan into motion. She pointed at the counter where a stand with a colorful sign stood proclaiming "Happy Birthday, Benji!" He was presented with his special pin which he wore proudly all day. He still smiles when he remembers the tour guide referring to him as "Benji" (Rosa's pet name for him that hardly anyone else uses). He used this moniker multiple times as he took us around the ice cream manufacturing plant.

It is our hope as we build our own family legend that our kids will do the same for our grandchildren to come. We hope we will be invited along on some of these journeys, but some necessarily will be taken with their own family units, their own households.

We hope we have taught them a thing or two in the trip-taking. If not, we hope they will ask for our advice; as you may be able to tell, we have a few pointers to share.

To give you a glimpse of some of our chronicled memories, we include below some journal entries from the kids. They are from two worlds of content: the narrative and the personal/profound. The first type is the narrative. Here are our two kids' lenses on the same adventure day:

"Bryce Canyon & Zion National Parks" by Ella, age 7

We went to Bryce National Park. We saw a canyon and it was big and red and old. We climbed that tall canyon, we went down and up. It was so rocky the challenge was not going down, it was going up. It was long, it made us all tired. Was it long, yes. Was it hot, yes. Did I complain, no of course not. I know it was tiring and hot and long, but it was awesome. You should go there someday, you will have a blast! I went to Zion. We just passed through like it was no big deal.

"Bryce Canyon & Zion National Parks" by Danny, age 9

We went to Bryce. We saw people walking down it! We decided to do that, exactly that. It was hard, not so much the way down but the way up. We finished and headed for Zion. We got to Zion. It was nice. We took pictures, but it was just a drive by and my mom got her stamp in her passport. I don't have much to say about this because it was just a drive by.

Sometimes journal entries are more personal, even profound. We enjoy this type the most:

"A Toothy Muffin" by Ella, age 7

(written on our "Alaska" trip, shared with her 3rd grade class)

I took a shower and brushed my teeth. Then took my vitamins and went to join my brother and my dad for breakfast. As usual, my dad ordered for us. My dad got a blueberry muffin, my brother got a chocolate muffin. I got an English muffin, my mom got some toast. And we all got fruit. Me and my brother tried honeydew, but when I took a bite of my English muffin, my tooth came out and I mean seriously, best day EVER!

"A Patriots' Day Poem" by Danny, age 9

(written after our "Washington D.C." trip, read to his whole Elementary School)

My flag is located in Washington D.C. along with many other flags. We symbolize the United States of America. We symbolize tragic events such as 9-11 and amazing victories. We symbolize all the men and women who lost their lives fighting for our country. We are extremely proud to be American flags.

Getting Your Family on the Road/ Getting the Kids Involved

---

1. If you feel your time is melting away with your kids as they grow up too quickly, remember you are in the driver's seat when it comes to travel. Do not settle for the travel you have always taken, go out and explore the

nation. There are wonderful adventures to be had less than 100 miles from home and many more to be had outside this range.

2. Get creative. Plan surprises for the kids during your travels, big and small. When you are going to a Disney destination, they have suggestions for how to do this (autograph books, pins to exchange with staff members, character meetings over a meal, etc.) Bigger surprises may take advanced planning and even reservations. But the biggest surprises will be surprises for you too, so keep an open mind and, occasionally, splurge.

3. Use social media to chronicle your trip, aim for 1-2 postings per day and always include a picture. Remember to "check in" to key destinations, tweet at the handles you are visiting, and hashtag liberally while taking specific note on how the attraction signs instruct you to do this.

4. Journaling is important because it breaks up the day's action, allows your children to indicate their highlights of your trips, and becomes a document you can refer back to. Even though that historic attraction may be very memorable for you, the mime you passed on the way may be more meaningful to your kids. In planning your subsequent travel, you may want to look back at what your kids enjoyed the last time around to choose destinations and experiences.

5. Help your children sort out their memories. After each stop, with miles ahead of you on the road, ask each family member what they liked best about your most recent experience. This is a short, fun game. It gives each

traveler a chance to share and even influence what you will all remember about that last attraction.

6. Share the stories you collect with friends and family on social media, but do not stop there. We view raising our kids as a partnership with their teachers each year. These teachers will love reading your kids' content and maybe even love sharing it with the rest of the class or the entire school.

7. Keep pictures in easy-to-find folders on computers and on phones. These are great screen savers and may just inspire you to take the next trip a little sooner.

8. Tell your stories over and over. These cement the memories for the children and for you. Since you are having the adventures of your lifetime, you will want to remember these times in vivid detail. For family and friends, a few memorable stories will also make more of an impression than a listing of where you visited or a link to your Shutterfly account.

9. Try new things and enjoy new experiences with your kids. The kids enjoy trying new foods, conquering new states and cities, learning new information and experiencing new adventures. You will love seeing your kids learn and experience new things on a trip so keep an eye out for fresh ideas. Parents, feel free to enjoy these new experiences (for you too) right alongside your kids.

10. Put away any lingering doubts and pick up a few blank notebooks and your smart phones, you really need to get on the road. Just go and let your legendary adventures begin!

Chapter 8

Tips for Extreme Road Tripping

"Baby, I don't know why I go to extremes."

— *Billy Joel, I Go To Extremes*

WE WERE IN KANSAS on a Friday; this was day 8 of our road trip. We had breakfast plans with family at home on Monday morning and could have very easily taken our time, gotten a hotel room somewhere in Ohio, and made it home with plenty of time for our Labor Day breakfast. We looked at each other and decided we just wanted to go home. This would mean traveling over 1,200 miles which translates to approximately twenty hours of driving.

We have gotten very good at managing this type of extreme travel. To travel 1,200 miles in one stretch means sleep-sharing, eating on the go, and only stopping for bathroom breaks and re-filling the car with gas. This type of travel is not for everyone and can be dangerous if all of the drivers are too tired to be alert on the road. In this particular case, though, we had been on the road for a while and had become accustomed to the rhythm of the long drive, we were both somewhat rested, and we could take on the challenge. We were home by late Sunday afternoon.

When we started out on our adventures, we did not plan to go to extremes. It was the constraints of our travel that dictated how we would travel. We had limited vacation time and we had to schedule our trips around school vacations so that the kids would not miss a single day. We had an end goal: to see all the states by car that we possibly could before the kids left for college. Extreme road tripping allowed us to accomplish our task far more quickly, a full eight years ahead of our initial plan.

After a number of shorter journeys, we did find we were extreme road trippers at heart. Extreme travel (here defined as averaging more than 10 hours of driving per day on a trip at least three days long) is how we have managed to drive to Seattle and back in nine days, California and back in ten days, and one time to Michigan and back over 72 hours without any real stop for sleep.

The advice we have offered so far is for road tripping of all types: short, medium or long, to the extreme or not. We ask that you consider what elements of a great trip are important to your family with the time and budget constraints that you have at home. You do not need to explore the entire United States nor do you have to travel exclusively by car. If you can afford periodic air travel, there are ways to see the lower 48 states more quickly than we have. You may also choose to stay closer to home, becoming a family of experts on your own unique region of the country.

In case you want to venture into extreme road tripping with your family, we have quite a few tips to ease your journeys. At least once, try to road trip to the extreme and see if your family relishes this type of journey or dislikes it. We have friends and family who tell us they would love to join us on our trips and others who thank us for not taking them along. We enjoy road trips to the extreme with lofty goals that push our own limits. For us, an extreme family road trip leaves us exhausted, but more excited to travel yet again, to the extreme.

Extreme traveling means utilizing resources of time and money carefully and fully. Time and money resources are interconnected. Every additional day on a road trip necessitates more meals, gas, hotels and attractions, all of which add to the total trip cost. We have discovered several tips and tricks that allow you to maximize time on the road safely and make an extreme road trip particularly more enjoyable.

While you are driving, **use your vehicle's cruise control**. You will be traveling through at least one night and whizzing through more than one day. It is important to keep your speed up while adhering to the posted speed limits. Without cruise control, you are likely to travel too fast at some points, but, especially at night, you are just as likely to go far under the speed limit as the road ahead goes on and on with no other car in sight to guide your own speed.

The first type of offense (driving too fast) can lead to a memorable and expensive traffic ticket while the second (driving too slow) takes you off your time course. For long drives, this can be a significant delay. We typically will set our cruise control to 3 or 4 miles per hour above the speed limit. This is safe (it does not merit a police stop) but given this first limitation, minimizes the travel time and gets you to your next destination faster.

Beware, however, that cruise control does reduce your attention to the drive. You must blast the radio or open a window to let in a flood of fresh air on occasion. Caffeinate often on the road. Listen to a great audio book or two. Converse with your passengers. Keep yourself alert while knowing you are traveling at great speed on your way to adventure.

The simplest way to save time on the road is to minimize stops whenever possible. This means traveling nonstop until you reach your first attraction. To accomplish this **you have to learn to sleep-share.** By this we mean that one of you is awake (and driving) and the other drivers are asleep, charging up for their turn on the next leg of the trip. Bring a pillow and blanket for the person or people sleeping. Take a sleep mask for daytime sleeping. We cannot stress this enough. At least one of you must be well-rested if you are planning to drive for more than eight hours on a stretch without significant stops.

Switch drivers before you are too tired to drive. If you find your eye lids drooping, you have been driving for too long. If all of the drivers in the car are too tired to drive, stop the car. Find a rest stop or a hotel room and take a break before continuing. Do not be a "hero" and try to drive past your own limits. We have been in situations where we were both too tired to drive. We then stopped in rest stops and got some fitful minutes of sleep until one of us was energized enough to continue on the road.

When you are on a road trip, there is almost no more welcoming sign than the one indicating there is a rest stop coming up soon. This is especially true when the driver of the vehicle is exhausted, feels the call of nature beckoning, or when one of the kids suddenly remembers they need "to go" when there was no rest stop sign in sight.

We have found not all rest stops are the same. Our favorite stops are ones just off the road we are using and include rest rooms, restaurants, gift shops and gas. Many states have rest stops that offer rest rooms, picnic areas and vending machines. Some rest stops are simple, short strips of road lined with semi-trailers with sleeping truckers inside the cabs. These oases provide a very necessary service on our country's roads.

Some rest stops are more robust and give you and your family a chance to rest and refuel your car. Others offer only the opportunity to stop, stretch and recharge yourselves. We have stopped in truck stops that have showers available for the weary traveler. Look out for the rest stop signs along the way. Most of the signs will clearly state whether the rest stop includes amenities such as vending machines, restaurants or gas.

We have encountered some rest stops that have a "closed" sign on them. This can happen, but have no fear: another rest stop will be available some miles down the road. There are apps available such as USA Rest Stop Locator that can be used to locate the nearest rest stop to your location on federal and state highways. You can also consult InterstateRestAreas.com if you want to include rest stop locations in your pre-trip planning phase or while on the road.

You may need to drive through more than one night and this requires careful coordination between the drivers. Unless you are committed to extreme road tripping, you should sleep in a bed each night. But if the road is calling you and there are seemingly countless miles ahead, make sure the passenger is sleeping while the driver drives. This makes the passenger much more awake when his or her turn comes. Plan in advance when the switch-offs will occur.

In our most extreme road travel to date, we spent 72 hours on the road and did not stop for sleep once. This was a difficult trip and we nearly ended the trip before the first stop. Early in the trip, we decided to continue to a nearby, unplanned stop: Hershey Chocolate World. It was literally on our way (with multiple signs on the Pennsylvania Turnpike pointing this way) and a quick check on Google showed the attraction was open.

Rosa wanted to head back and rest at home, let the road win this one time. The other three of us wanted to press on, but this meant not stopping for a hotel. Such a stop would be a deal-breaker with too much temptation to head home after a night's rest.

We drove all the way to a canoe shack on the west coast of Michigan and canoed for a few blissful hours in nearby waters. We then went on to Holland, Michigan and visited the Dutch village right off the highway there. Then we drove straight home. In a drive like this, it was important to rest for 30-45 minutes a few times on the road in designated rest stops.

An important tip for the extreme road tripper: **if you must stop at a rest stop for some "car hotel" sleep, do it**. This is a last resort; lock the doors and park with other cars basically doing the same thing. By the time you are considering such a move, you really need some rest though this will not be quality sleep, just a quick boost.

Another recommendation we have for extreme family road tripping: **plan your stops carefully and maximize these stops**. There is a near-constant temptation on the road to stop. Restaurants look good, the gas gauge demands frequent attention, passengers will need bathroom breaks and sleep can seem essential (largely because it is).

We recommend you make stops for all of these reasons, but do so with a plan. When we are driving, we typically pick a particular time to stop. If we have a 6 hour drive ahead, we will usually plan to stop 3 or 4 hours into this drive. At the stop, we will get caffeine in some form, we will all go to the bathroom, we will pick up a snack or even a meal, and we will take a family selfie if the occasion merits it. Once we stop halfway through a long drive, we do not want to stop again until we reach our destination.

A great stop on our second trip to Los Angeles was Ozarkland which, the billboards assured us, is a "Road Trip Tradition" (we got a few "traditional" family selfies there). We stopped and browsed the gift shop, got two types of delicious fudge from the counter, got gas at a nearby gas station and stopped at a McDonald's for food and a family bathroom break. Despite three stops on this road trip pause, we accomplished all we needed to with only 45 minutes off-road. Kingdom City, Missouri (despite not being a planned stop) will live on in our memories as a great set of short stops along the way to a record trip.

Visits with family and friends can be incredibly enjoyable on a long road trip, but for the extreme road tripping family, remember: **your family and friends need to fit into your trip plan**. When visiting our cousins in Santa Cruz, we had time for a meal (a great 3-hour stop where we met our newest cousin, baby Elliott, for the first time). When visiting our friend Lynn in Los Angeles, we had time again for a meal (a superb Denny's breakfast) and then we were off to Disneyland. In this case, Lynn was very willing to join us at the Park (she had packed a bag in advance), so we extended our time with her, much to our and the kids' delight. Lynn had visited Disneyland many times before and was a wonderful tour guide.

When visiting one of Rosa's friends, Jamie, and her boyfriend near Seattle, we had time for coffee and some breakfast. Jamie suggested the *Twin Peaks* diner about 30 minutes outside of the city and only a few minutes away from our chosen hotel. We had some cherry pie and a great cup of coffee (or, as the television show states, a "damn good" cup of coffee). We picked up a souvenir mug from the diner and remember that visit every time we use it. When visiting with friends on the road, it is a great idea to let them suggest the meeting place. They know the lay of the land.

Sometimes the timing or route does not allow for visiting. We have had to decline a few attractive offers along the way because logistics did not work. You may have noticed, however, that **since you need to stop and eat, this can be a perfect time to get together with close by locals who can suggest a unique stopping place**.

When not visiting friends and relatives, you will still need to eat on the road as a family. Sit-down restaurants will take a minimum of two hours out of your trip between getting seated, ordering, eating and using the restroom. The best way to save the time of stopping to eat on the road is to pre-pack a few meals and have them ready in the car.

Another way is a little more time-consuming. Multitask by grabbing a quick meal at the convenience store while gassing up the car. You can also opt for a drive-through meal at a fast food restaurant. That option is even faster than a gas station convenience store as long as the drive thru window line is not too long.

Remember to pace yourself according to what mileage you can accomplish on any day of your road trip. On the way back from a long trip to Seattle, we simply could not manage a 15-hour drive day. We decided to make an unplanned stop in Fort Wayne, Indiana where we took in a wonderful reenactment weekend at the Fort. We also made an unplanned stop in Columbus, Ohio where we enjoyed room service for the first and only time ever in a Crowne Plaza; since the hotel caters to business travelers during the work week, we got a great weekend rate through our Expedia app for one night.

Sometimes, you will be ahead of schedule and you will need an extra day on the road. Use it. You do not get points for early arrival at the expense of your family's sanity or health. Sometimes the unplanned stops of a trip are also the most memorable; there are points for that!

Remember the time you have allocated to each stop along your route. Many people we tell our stories to cannot imagine the short time we spend at each stop along our route. Frequently, the quip has been "so you drive up, take a picture and keep moving, huh?" Sometimes, this is quite true. On our first stop ever in Wichita, Kansas, we stopped for scrumptious barbeque and asked the locals behind the counter where we should go to "see something" in the city. They suggested the Keeper of the Plains statue nearby. After a short drive, we saw the beautiful monument and, you guessed it, we took a few quick pictures before heading back east toward home.

After a long drive westward during a later trip, again in Kansas, we took a picture with a humongous Buffalo Bill statue outside a closed museum in Oakley. Sometimes pictures are actually a perfect family memory. On this particular stop, we took turns taking pictures with another family that had stopped for the same photo opportunity.

Most times, however, we will budget 3-4 hours for a major stop. This means thinking about the highlight reel in advance: which points along the way will make this attraction memorable? In Mesa Verde, we kept stopping at various historical sites from as far back as 600 A.D. and at various overlooks along the way. With so many stops, however, we opted not to take any of the ranger-led tours which, though modestly priced, would cost us more precious time.

Some stops, like a Disney park, however, require a full 8-14 hours; do not short-change these key, family-friendly destinations. Allocate a full day into your initial plan. The expense of this single day at Disney, and the multitude of amazing attractions, make the full day time investment worthwhile.

Use our advice to pack your car well with plenty of snacks, entertainment and comfortable sleep gear. This will eliminate the need for some stops. Also, remember to recap each day for your kids and for yourselves. You do not want the days blending together on your trip, there is too much excitement going on for that. Extreme road tripping inherently requires you to experience attractions at a rather speedy clip. This means if you do not stop to take stock of where you have been and what you did, you could potentially miss enjoying the moments altogether. Keep the kids engaged and use writings and social media posts to recount your trips for day-of and later review.

You can always read back journals or scroll backward through your social media feeds to savor a stop you made while somewhat sleep-deprived. You may find a particular brand of entertainment is not working (you cannot seem to hold on to the audio book story or no channels on the radio seem to offer anything of interest). If you find your mind wandering, switch to some other form of entertainment to keep yourself engaged and awake. You can always rewind that last chapter of the audio book or start your search anew for a radio station with one of your favorite songs.

In our case, only Rosa started out liking country music. Since country music is so prevalent in most of the country, however, there are times where country stations are the only available options. For this reason, after several cross-country trips, we have all become country music fans. The kids particularly like the Rodney Atkins song *Watching You* and like to remind Ben they are each his "buckaroo."

Take time to enjoy local delicacies and customs. Take part in these memorable, regional delights as these can form strong sense-memories even when traveling to extremes. In Holland, Michigan, this meant trying on different pairs of wooden shoes at the Dutch village. In New Orleans, this was walking the streets in the French Quarter and savoring beignets at Café du Monde. In Colonial Williamsburg, we ate at a true-to-the-period tavern and sampled the "olde" cuisine. In the American southwest, we tried all kinds of animal jerky. In Cleveland, Ohio, we tried the very unique Skyline Chili on the recommendation of several natives. In Juneau, we had to try Alaskan King crab at Tracy's King Crab Shack just as we had to try the Alaskan salmon lunch atop Mount Roberts.

In Kentucky, the adults tried strong bourbon after touring the Buffalo Trace Distillery while the kids enjoyed their own equivalent, root beer. In New Hampshire, Vermont and Quebec we all tried the local maple syrup (by drinking it!). In Quebec, make sure to test out whatever level of French you may know; Ben highly enjoyed recovering some of his own high-school "fluency." Another favorite Quebec delight is frozen maple syrup on a stick. The syrup is poured over fresh snow, rolled on a popsicle stick and eaten while it drips down. The tiny ice crystals mix with the sweet, sticky candy that forms and the result is an amazingly sweet, sensational treat. In each case, we can still taste the deliciousness of the regional cuisine and have fond cultural experiences to remember as a family.

A final tip for the extreme road tripping family: **find special experiences where you are traveling, even if these are available in some form at home**. Having these adventures on the road adds a layer of excitement. On one trip, we stopped in Indiana for dine-in theater. We watched the latest installment of the *Star Wars* series where Kylo Ren is first introduced. It was a pricey, but enjoyable experience to dine well amidst this chapter of the movie legend. As we researched a way to repeat this experience, it turns out the same thing is available about 45 minutes from our home. That said, this first experience in the middle of Indiana on a long car odyssey was much more memorable than it would have been closer to home.

On our trip to New Hampshire, which turned out to be in the off-season, we called our hotel and asked what we could do during our vacation. They did not have too many ideas, it was "between seasons" they explained. They did suggest we check out what the local chamber of commerce had to offer. Not having too much hope for this avenue, we were very pleased to find a rendition of *The Lorax* was being performed nearby. This was an amazing experience with an acted-out, costumed reading of the book including a multitude of snacks that were all Lorax-themed. The price of admission was to bring one book per child and the play included a free pancake breakfast. We then took a fun nature hike on the theater grounds.

Despite how much we enjoyed this stop, we had already read *The Lorax* and had seen the movie at home. It is also likely we could have found a similar theater experience near home, since close by Philadelphia and New York City are both known for having many excellent theaters. Nevertheless, the New Hampshire stop was a wonderful, family-fun experience. The kids referred to this stop for months afterward as their favorite adventure stop. You never know when visiting a place in the off-season, with some advance research of course, will lead to triumph.

Getting Your Family on the Road/ Getting the Kids Involved

1. Extreme road travel (defined as averaging more than 10 driving hours per day on a trip at least three days long) can be fun even with kids, give it a try!

2. Keep in mind your family constraints at home, especially time and budget considerations. Extreme road travel is a perfect choice when you are looking to maximize adventure and mileage while minimizing the total cost of a trip.

3. To maximize your drive time, use your vehicle's cruise control. Set this at 3-4 miles per hour above the posted speed limit to avoid police intervention, but nevertheless travel the furthest your time will allow. When using cruise control, compensate with in-car entertainment to keep your mind extra alert.

4. Learn to sleep-share when road tripping to the extreme. This means while the driver is driving and all are exhausted, the other drivers must sleep to be alert for their turn at the wheel.

5. If there are no drivers that can continue on the journey, stop the car at hotels or motels when these fit into the plan. As an emergency measure, pull into a rest stop and recharge for 30-45 minutes until one driver can safely continue the trek forward.

6. Maximize stops along your route to fuel up, get needed snacks or a meal, use the bathroom and even get some sleep. Plan stopping points in advance at midway points during longer drives on your trip. This gives the driver a certain "time" goal in mind to get to that next stop and pushes all of you further into the journey.

7. Visiting family and friends on the road can be very enjoyable and memorable, but make sure these visits fit into your travel plan. Whenever possible, let them pick meeting places that are unique and convenient; they know the local landscape far better than you do.

8. Take time to enjoy local delicacies and unique experiences. Whether it is trying on a pair of wooden shoes in Holland, Michigan or tasting the straight-from-the-barrel bourbon in Lexington, Kentucky, these sense-memories will be very strong even once your return home.

9. Find special experiences when you are traveling, even if these may be available closer to home. For kids especially, a theater performance or dine-in movie can be even more enjoyable while on the road. Remember to recap each

stop and each day's adventure with your kids so the days on an extreme trek do not blend together.

10. Discard any lingering worries about extreme road travel and get on the road. Just go, commit to one extreme road trip to see if your family savors the unique experience. Let your extreme adventure begin!

Chapter 9

Parks and Recreation

"We believed in our idea—a family park where parents
and children could have fun—together."

— *Walt Disney*

WHILE PLANNING OUR ROUTES in the quest to drive to all
the contiguous United States, we spent many hours researching possible destinations. It is not always easy to find an
attraction all of us will like. Between the four of us, we have several attraction types we each prefer and not all of them overlap.

We have a few go-to destinations, however, that we can all
agree on. If any route we are traveling has an especially famous
National Park or monument, we are more likely to find a way to
sew that destination into our trip tapestry. We have discovered
several helpful tips to add to the experiences of these destina-

tions and have found a few cost-saving methods as well. When we considered Florida, the first destination we unanimously agreed upon was Disney World in Orlando.

Several years ago, we parents sat across the table from each other sharing a nice bottle of champagne and celebrating our 9th wedding anniversary. We summed up the year that had passed, took inventory of our adventures, and tried to decide what our next adventure would look like. By this point, it seemed that most of our kids' friends had visited at least one of the Disney parks and our kids had not. Our first thought was the trip would be too expensive and out of reach.

The typical Disney trip, we observed, lasted approximately one week. This meant seven days at roughly $1,000 per day for the four of us. Nevertheless, we decided the kids simply must go to Disney and we needed to get them there. We would need to make this trip work in the short-term when the whimsical magic of Disney comes alive for younger ones. We researched our options and came up with an affordable, yet still magical, game plan.

The first challenge we faced with a Disney vacation was the cost. How would we get to experience the wonder of Disney without breaking the bank? To start, we considered the cost of various transportation options and even looked into overnight trains to get us from New Jersey to Florida and back. After some research, we returned to what we already knew: driving four people would be far less expensive than flying or any other option. The first decision was made, we would drive.

The next item we considered was time at the park. The more days you spend at Disney, the higher the cost. For instance, the cost of visiting the Magic Kingdom is around $100 per day per person. For our family of four, this means a little over $400 per day just for park admission before we consider food and hotel accommodations. The other Disney park admission rates are slightly less than $100 per day per person, while a "park hopper" pass (which allows you to visit multiple parks) is closer to $130 per day per person.

We decided we would visit one park this time and would only spend one day exploring it. Since this was a first visit for both kids and they were still small (8 and 6 years old), we chose the Magic Kingdom. We felt the Magic Kingdom was the ideal way to introduce the kids to Disney, with its classic Disney rides including "It's a Small World" (Mom and Dad each have fond memories of this ride from their own childhoods) and its classic Disney heroes and villains.

We looked up AAA discounts and online offers, but finally called the official Disney customer service number. Disney offers wonderful package deals and their customer service representatives (referred to as cast members along with all the other employees) are courteous and very helpful. It turned out the package offered by our cast member was comparable to the one AAA had.

We considered staying at a motel outside the park at first. After speaking with the Disney cast member and visiting the Disney website, however, we learned about economy options on Disney properties. Hotels such as "All-Star Sports" and "All-Star

Movies" are very reasonably priced. These no-frill hotel options are inexpensive, but still come with the benefits you would get with the more costly choices. Both the Sports and Music resorts are fun to walk around with your kids and have great outdoor pools.

We did discover these resorts tend to cater to families with no more than four people, unless the fifth person is an infant. Disney policy is these rooms are not big enough for more than the four and, for fire safety reasons, they will not allow you to book them if your party is larger. This is something to consider if you have more than four people in your party. There are a few rooms that can accommodate a larger group, but these rooms are in the more expensive Disney hotels.

When staying at a Disney resort, a meal plan (prepaid snacks and full meals for each day of your stay) can be added to the package of your entire trip. **This is a significant benefit because the meal plan gives you access to fun eating experiences and saves you a great deal of money.** Outside food and beverages are not allowed in the park, which means you have to purchase meals and drinks while in the park or leave the park to eat. Disney park restaurants and eateries are also exceedingly expensive unless you have your meal plan set ahead of time.

The meal plan includes a colorful, plastic travel mug for each member of the family. These mugs have a microchip in them that allows unlimited refills for the duration of the meal plan. Though you are not permitted to bring these mugs into the park, they can be used at designated Disney resorts (get the mugs as soon as you check in for maximum usage). The travel mugs are fun and very well made. We still use them as travel mugs at home years later. It is also always fun to walk by a co-worker in the break room who is carrying his or her own Disney travel mug. These mugs have sparked many amusing Disney adventure conversations at the office.

A favorite meal option of ours is the Disney character meal. Several restaurants, some in the Disney parks and some outside the parks, offer meals that include certain Disney characters who will come to your table and interact with you while you eat. This is a great opportunity for the kids to collect autographs and get their picture taken with their favorite Disney characters. **These character meals book up fast so make sure to make reservations well in advance. Take special note not to book character meals within parks you do not have tickets to; you cannot come in just for the meal.** The cast member you make the vacation reservation with can help you with these special meal reservations as well. A list of available character meals and additional details can be found on the Disney website.

Once the vacation is booked, you will have an option to download the Disney App on a smart phone or tablet. This App will allow you to check into your hotel room online which is a great way to avoid standing in line for a room. You can also choose your initial Fast Passes (legal line jumping on certain rides) on the App as well as make meal reservations including character meals. The Fast Pass is a timed entry to a ride or show; you will have a window of time in which to come to the attraction entrance and be allowed in without having to stand in the regular line.

You will be able to choose fast passes for three attractions at first. Once you use these fast passes, you can choose another by checking in at one of the fast pass kiosks located in the park. You will only be able to choose one fast pass at a time at this point and you will not be able to get another until the window of the fast pass you selected has elapsed. Any cast member can point you to the nearest fast pass kiosk. **Fast pass management is an important strategy if you only have a single day to conquer a Disney park in either Florida or California.**

When selecting your fast passes, it is helpful to know which rides need them and which ones have shorter wait lines. The Disney App will show you the rides at the park and give you real-time wait times. If you check into the wait time section of the app before you select your fast passes, you can get a good idea of which fast passes you should choose based on which rides have the longest wait times. Check the wait times at several points during the day as they can change significantly.

You will also be able to use the Disney App to choose the colors of the "magic band" bracelets that will be sent to you in advance by mail. These bracelets will unlock your hotel room door and allow you entry into the park while keeping track of your fast passes. The bracelets will be scanned in lieu of payment when purchasing food at the park and will keep track of your meal plan credits. When getting your picture taken by the professional Disney photographers at the park, your bracelet will be scanned and the pictures transfer to your online Disney account. You can purchase a photo package to go with your Disney package or go online and purchase pictures à la carte.

Disneyland in California does not utilize the magic bands, but the park does offer fast pass options as well. You can use your entrance ticket at the fast pass kiosks available around the park and you will get a slip of paper with your fast pass. You do not have the option to get more than one fast pass at a time, but we found this limit was not a problem as long as we timed our passes just right.

A long-time Disney adventuring friend told us about the pin exchange at Disney. The pin exchange is the tradition of exchanging official Disney pins with cast members in the Disney parks. Pins can be purchased at an exorbitant price on the Disney web site, at Disney stores or at the parks. **A better option is to purchase a large quantity of pins on Amazon or eBay ahead of time at a small fraction of the cost.**

Once you have your inexpensive starter kit of pins, take them to the park and find a cast member with a lanyard covered in Disney pins. You can choose any of the pins the cast member has and exchange it for one of the pins you have. Sometimes the cast members will wear their pins backward so the final reveal is a surprise. Almost always when you bring little ones, the cast members will make a show of bending down to kid-level to complete the transaction. Our kids loved the pin exchange. When we went to Epcot a year later, we took our collection of pins and continued the game.

We applied our extreme road trip theme to our first Disney experience. We left New Jersey in the evening and drove through the night, arriving in Florida late the next morning. We checked into our All-Star Movie Disney resort in the late afternoon and received "1st Visit" Disney buttons. There was a voice message on the phone from Goofy welcoming the kids. This is something Danny still brings up. It made a big impression on him and was a delightful surprise for all of us.

We brought costumes with us to Disney. Ellie wanted to wear an Anna costume from Disney's *Frozen*, and Danny wanted to be a pirate. If you have some extra time in Disney, the Magic Kingdom has a princess makeover experience as well as a pirate makeover experience. This takes about half a day and is rather expensive. **Bringing your own costumes allows your kids to enjoy a similar experience at a fraction of the cost.** We have yet to try the official Disney makeover offerings, but we hear from friends it is worth the time and money (if you budget for both).

Our first character meal was wonderful. We rested for a bit in our hotel room and went to an early dinner nearby at the Disney Swan hotel. Goofy and Pluto joined us at that meal and the kids got their autographs and some fun, posed pictures. We had reserved an early dinner time which meant we had the characters almost to ourselves for a good 20 minutes. When you visit Disney hotels, even for a meal, poking around the grounds is an attraction in and of itself. Always take time to peruse the resort grounds if you can.

The next day we checked out of our hotel and headed for the park. Since we drove to Florida in our own car, we did not have to use shuttles. We were determined to maximize our one day and found a fantastic parking spot when we arrived early. We spent the whole day at the Magic Kingdom, managing to ride almost all the rides at the park (this is possible even with small children).

We had dinner at the Cinderella character meal which was an even better experience than the day before. The food was more kid-friendly and five different characters from Cinderella came to our table to interact with the kids. We have the most spectacular picture of Ella standing next to Prince Charming. The look on her face is precious and conveys the most adorable expression of "I cannot believe I am standing next to Prince Charming."

We headed out of the park right after the evening light show on Cinderella's castle and got home by the next afternoon. The total expense for that trip was less than $1,500 for the four of us. On this limited budget, the trip was a great first foray into the amazing world of Disney.

A final note about Disneyland versus Disneyworld. Disneyland is the original theme park; Mr. Walt Disney himself walked the streets of Disneyland. This park is smaller and therefore more manageable, but there are roughly the same number of rides as in the Florida park. The thrill rides are more friendly for those of us who are not thrill-seekers (Mom). Even Rosa enjoyed the roller coaster offerings at Disneyland, including the flume ride. The speed and thrill level were just right by being more kid-sized.

"One touch of nature makes the whole world kin."

— *John Muir, Our National Parks*

We have enjoyed nearly every stop at National Parks along our journeys. The first National Park we selected as a destination was Mount Rushmore. This landmark was a major deciding factor in that particular road trip, the one where we reached Seattle. We wanted to travel with the kids for at least one week of the summer vacation. This was our most daring trip at that point, our first cross-country odyssey with kids. In that case, nine days of road travel took us from one coast of the country to the other and back.

We had the vacation time and the kids were already off school for the summer, but did we want to spend nine days on the road (nearly double the travel time of our longest, previous trip)? We considered our options. We could take a shorter trip or maybe take the kids on a cruise. After weighing these options and long discussions, we kept coming back to the fact that neither of us had seen Mount Rushmore and now we had the time to drive there, we really needed to go and see it.

It did not disappoint. We had seen images of the monument in books, movies, television and photographs, but nothing compared to driving up to the Black Hills and seeing it in person. In fact, there is a moment in driving when you suddenly see four faces in the rock and it takes you totally by surprise since you are still a few miles away. The park itself is beautifully manicured with lovely walking trails and several picturesque viewing points that make for wonderful photo ops.

One of our favorite pictures was of Danny holding up a vanilla ice cream cone in such a way that it looked like he was sharing it with President Jefferson. This picture was taken based on a

Twitter prompt (#jeffersonicecream) from the ice cream parlor on the premises. They retweeted us promptly which added to the thrill of the visit.

The ice cream was also delicious (vanilla is the favorite flavor of both Danny and Jefferson) with generous portions. We highly recommend a visit to Memorial Team Ice Cream when you visit Mount Rushmore. Also, know the National Park Service is very active on Twitter. #NPS or #FindYourPark on your Twitter posting will likely get your family a retweet and even a picture posted on their main website, FindYourPark.com.

Mount Rushmore has a wonderful Junior Ranger program. This is an offering you can find in most of the National Park locations. The Park Rangers have booklets that are geared to different age groups usually marked by different animals to signal different levels of difficulty. **Rangers have always been more than happy to present the Junior Ranger books and go over instructions with the kids.** The booklets encourage kids to investigate the park. Some of the sections require the kids to find answers to questions by studying the park itself. Other sections of the booklet ask questions which point the kids to the Visitor Center museum.

There are Junior Ranger books that direct the kids to talk to a Ranger or attend at least one Ranger-led discussion or tour. Our favorite Ranger-led discussion happened when we ducked into a remodeled tower at the Grand Canyon in surprise torrential rain. A young Ranger got an idea for his captive audience, trying to kill time with the rain pouring outside. It was time for a geology lesson.

It turns out Bryce Canyon, Zion and the Grand Canyon are all related, part of the same geologic region. Bryce Canyon is at the top which feeds into (lower on the rock landscape) Zion which feeds into the Grand Canyon. We were at that moment at the bottom of the geologic landscape with the mighty Colorado River cutting through the Grand Canyon rock at a rate of paper-thin erosion every year. This information brought an interesting narrative into this particular trip where we had visited Bryce, Zion and Grand Canyon coincidentally in that order. We had traveled a full geologic landscape hundreds of millions of years in the making all in just a few days.

Back to the activity books, though, we love helping the kids find answers to the questions. This is a great way for us parents to learn about each park as well. Once the booklets are completed, the kids have to return them to a Ranger. The Ranger then instructs the kids take an oath. Every Ranger has his or her own style, but the general idea of the oath is to respect the parks and nature.

Each Ranger has added some personal flair to this oath. Our favorite addition was the one making the kids swear not to fight in the car for the rest of the trip. Other Rangers included a promise to help around the house with chores or pick up litter in the parks. Once the oath is administered, the Ranger signs off on the booklet, which the kids get to keep, and hands each one a golden, plastic Junior Ranger badge. Some National Parks give the option of iron-on patches and some even have Girl and Boy Scout patches for kids who are part of a troop.

We discovered another fun National Park tradition while investigating the Welcome Center at Scotts Bluff in Nebraska. We purchased a National Parks Passport. The passport includes all of the National Parks, National Monuments, and National Historic Sites in the United States. The states in the passport are broken into clusters, and each cluster has a numbered list of locations that correspond to numbers on the color-coded maps in each section. The sections include pictures and descriptions of some of the numbered locations as well.

In addition to the wonderful information within the National Parks Passport, there are blank boxes provided for filling with stamps and seals. The stamps and seals can be found in the various main Welcome Centers at the parks. Seals can be purchased and the stamps are free. The kids love taking turns pressing the stamp in the ink pad and stamping a fresh image into the passport. Just walk into any National Park Welcome Center and ask a Ranger for the stamp. The Ranger will direct you to the designated area where the park stamps are located by an ink pad.

This area is sometimes located in the Welcome Center gift shop where you can find the seals as well. You will sometimes find small slips of paper by the stamps. These slips of paper are handy if you have forgotten your passport. Just stamp the slip of paper and glue the paper into your passport when you get back to it. **We have found ourselves with some extra time on some of our journeys and have flipped through the National Park Passport for destination ideas.** We have found some terrific attractions this way.

The best surprise to date while traveling was the Aztec Ruins National Monument. When the words "Aztec Ruins" left Rosa's mouth, Ben's eyebrows perked (it was like being told there was a second, more excitingly-named "Roswell"). The name alone sold it, though the name does turn out to be problematic. Aztec Ruins was incorrectly named "Aztec" and the site is not considered "ruins" by the Pueblo peoples whose ancestors actually built them.

Putting nomenclature issues aside, however, we got to explore 3 kivas (holy gathering houses) restored on site and walked as a family through many of the dwellings, going through short doorways and touching some 1,000-year-old rocks that have been nicely restored. The site is in move-in condition except the roofs are off so you are fully exposed to the elements, white lizards are everywhere and, for our tastes, the rooms do not boast much privacy.

But since we did not need to move in, we got up close and took a self-guided tour of about 45 minutes. Incredible and beautiful, we took dozens of pictures in this short time period. The museum was full of Junior Ranger clues and our little ones, for the third time during that particular trip, were sworn in as Junior Rangers. Among the interesting facts surrounding the site, the outside wall of the compound was built to correspond exactly to the rising sun's path during the Summer Solstice. Great, celestial architecture.

The price of admission to National Parks is very reasonable and you have the option of purchasing an annual National Parks pass for around $80. There are also several times per year when the National Parks offer free admission. The weekend closest to August 25th, the National Parks' birthday, is one of those times. This date falls during the kids' summer vacation and is an excellent time to take the family on a trip to one of the many beautiful and exciting options located throughout the United States. One summer, we visited 3 different parks during one of these weekends without knowing this was a free weekend in advance. All of the free entrance days to National Parks can be found on the NPS.gov website along with additional, helpful information.

Getting Your Family on the Road/ Getting the Kids Involved

1. At Disney, the best part about staying "on resort" is the meal plan. This is an affordable way to enjoy entertaining Disney-style dining on your trip and comes with stylish take-home mugs that will trigger fond memories for many years afterword.

2. Character meals are fun dining experiences with kid-friendly food and photo opportunities sure to make your social media feeds. Make sure to do the research, plan well in advance and book these meals from home to get your top picks.

3. The Disney App is free and useful for checking into your resort hotel room, checking ride times and choosing initial fast passes, and generally getting you excited about your upcoming trip. Download the App as soon as you book your vacation.

4. Fast passes are extremely important if you will be pressed for time at any Disney park. If you are going to conquer a

park in a single day, fast passes will maximize the number of rides that your family can experience.

5. Pins and costumes both create unique and fun memories for your kids at Disney parks. Purchasing both in advance allows you to save money and valuable time at the park.

6. National Parks are particularly active on Twitter. Hashtag #FindYourPark and #NPS when it makes sense on Twitter and keep an eye out for Twitter prompts while you visit the Parks.

7. Junior Ranger booklets are a wonderful way for kids and adults to condense learning at National Parks and have some fun while searching for clues and answers together. Once complete, your little ones will enjoy being sworn in as Junior Rangers and will have shiny, plastic badges to showcase their accomplishment.

8. National Park Passports are great for marking where you have visited and wonderful for discovering new National Parks available on your route.

9. Check out NPS.gov for helpful tips on the National Parks you plan to visit and be on the lookout for free days and weekends.

10. Take your National Park Passport and your Disney pixie dust and get on the road. Just go and let the magical and natural wonder take you away!

Chapter 10

Space and Time

"Time and space are not conditions in which we live, but modes by which we think."

— *Albert Einstein*

WE BELIEVE A GOOD education does not have to be relegated to the conventional classroom. Our adventures around the United States have presented us with a plethora of educational opportunities for kids and adults alike. In addition to exploring natural wonders and extraordinary theme parks, we have found ways to experience the joys of space and time travel as a family.

By visiting the space centers that were built around the National Aeronautics and Space Administration (N.A.S.A.) programs and installations, we have learned about the past, present and future of space exploration. We have traveled back in time when visiting attractions where history has been recreated and reenacted; some stops have been permanent exhibits and others temporary events.

These attractions are fun and educational for all of us. Since many of these attractions will eventually relate to subjects the kids will be learning in school, we encourage them to be inquisitive and ask as many questions as they can. These attractions teach new information and can reinforce the school curriculum.

Some of our favorite moments are watching the kids make associations between what they are seeing and things they are learning in school. When we sit around the dinner table and ask the kids what they learned in school that day, most of the time their answers come in one-word retorts: math, spelling, sometimes even "nothing." When we stop at educational attractions on our family road trips, we are encouraged to discover they are learning so much more as they detail chunks of knowledge gained from their classrooms.

Ben and Ella are *Star Trek* fans. They have watched every episode of *Star Trek: The Next Generation*, and most of *Deep Space 9* together. Ella can name all the characters, their ranks and station or spaceship positions on these shows. The idea of space exploration appeals to all of us.

We were delighted to discover the Infinity Science Center, a N.A.S.A. museum, located within our trip route through Hancock County, Mississippi. When researching places to visit in Alabama, we found the U.S. Space and Rocket Center in Huntsville which became our target attraction. We enjoyed both experiences and we started looking for more opportunities to learn at the N.A.S.A. museums. About a year later, we stopped at Kennedy Space Center on our way to Epcot Center in Florida. You can find the N.A.S.A. museums and visitor centers on VisitNasa.com.

We reached the Infinity Science Center in Mississippi just before it opened and walked its grounds. This location is where N.A.S.A. built and tested the rockets that propelled space crafts into orbit and to the moon. The area surrounding the visitor center has a few of these rockets on display, as well as a lovely fountain and reflecting pool.

The museum itself is small compared to other N.A.S.A. centers, but interesting and informative. The part we enjoyed most was the bus tour of the grounds where we learned about early rocket testing and got to see actual sites where these tests took place. **When visiting the Infinity Science Center, enjoy the museum, but definitely make sure to take the bus tour.**

The next N.A.S.A. location we visited was the U.S. Space and Rocket Center in Huntsville, Alabama. This is a much larger museum than its Mississippi cousin. There are several visitor centers to visit, accessible with the complementary shuttle bus. We watched a wonderful film about senses at the IMAX Spacedome theater, watched the kids conquer a rock climbing wall, and enjoyed a fun simulation of a visit to Mars. The U.S. Space and Rocket Center hosts a summer space camp each year. This camp is not only for kids. The camp offers a program for adults 18 years old and up. If you have always dreamed of being an astronaut, this may be your chance to live that dream.

Here again, the highlight of our experience was taking N.A.S.A.'s Marshall Space Flight Center (MSFC) Bus Tour. One of the stops includes a visit to the command center for the International Space Station. This is where the U.S. astronauts in the space station communicate with Earth. If you are lucky enough to be on the tour when this communication takes place, you can witness the exchange yourself. There are times when astronauts are visiting the command center and will come out and speak with the tour as well.

If you need to, use the restrooms before going on this tour. The area is restricted and you will not be allowed to use the restrooms on site. Since you will be touring a restricted government base, only U.S. citizens are allowed to take this tour. Make sure to have valid identification with you for this visit.

There were five of us on this particular trip. Once we paid our admission, we were told that with the admission price we had paid, we would get two free admission tickets to the museum as well as an annual Association of Science—Technology Centers (ASTC) Travel Passport. This was a lovely, surprise perk and we were delighted to receive it. The ASTC Passport gives you free general admission to a wide variety of science centers. This list can be found on ASTC.org. The one stipulation for free admission with the Passport is the museums you go to cannot be closer than 90 miles from your place of residence. If they are within the designated "local area" you have to purchase tickets to enter.

The most polished of the N.A.S.A. attractions we have seen to date is Kennedy Space Center. The bus tour through generations of launching pads is both a tour through the history of the space program and a captivating journey of wonder. The Atlantis shuttle in mid-air in the museum is perhaps the most amazing thing we have seen in any museum on any of our road trips. Kennedy Space Center is best described as a combination of a theme park and a gigantic N.A.S.A. archive. One of our most memorable experiences there was meeting an astronaut, casually shaking his hand and exchanging a few words while getting our Kennedy Space Center brochure autographed by him for posterity. This "astronaut encounter" is a live event every day included with admission.

Kennedy Space Center offers a selection of fascinating lectures on a variety of space-related topics. We sat in on a lecture about the latest in-orbit telescope technology designed to explore the galaxy. Earlier that day, Ella asked us if we think there is life on other planets. We recalled the book we had listened to on the road by Stephen Hawking and his daughter describing the criteria for a planet that could sustain life. Apparently, many planets that have been found millions of light years away are great candidates to be life-sustaining planets. Ella approached the speaker after the lecture was complete and posed the same question to her: "Is there life on other planets?"

A fellow Kennedy Center guest overheard the conversation and added, "and do you think they have visited Earth?" This led to an intriguing chat in which we discussed the theories we had learned from Stephen Hawking. Our delightful lecturer listened to our thoughts and ideas and said she feels there must be intelligent life out there, but she believes they have yet to discover the technology that would allow them to come to Earth. We decided not to bring up our visit to Roswell, New Mexico and the mysterious carving of the Mayan Ancient Astronaut.

In our family road trips, we look for attractions that involve historical recreations and reenactments. We call these experiences "time-travel" and the events give a historical immersion experience. Many include actors who represent people of the time. These experts are knowledgeable and very adept at explaining and describing unique aspects of the area during the period. The kids love walking into a house or place of business and interacting with the characters. Most of the actors we have encountered take their job very seriously and rarely break character.

We look for three categories of time-travel attractions. In the first category are permanent exhibits that can be visited during most of the year. In the next are permanent live-action shows that take you back in time to one location for a short time. The final category includes temporary, annual reenactment events. In the rest of this chapter, we will give you ideas of what we have encountered and the types of exhibits, shows and events to be on the lookout for in your own travels.

We stopped at Living History Farms in Urbandale, Iowa on our cross-country trip to Seattle. This attraction offers a robust time-travel experience. The exhibits include a demonstration of Native American crop growing in the 1700s, a working farm from the early 1900s, and the charming little town of Walnut Hill circa 1875. Walnut Hill has a pretty amazing claim to fame: in 1979, Pope John Paul II visited the chapel housed in this town re-creation and held mass for 350,000 people right there.

We started our tour in the town. There were several houses to investigate complete with inhabitants in period garb who gave us a tour and a history lesson. One of the houses had several chickens milling about in the back yard. These chickens let us get close enough to pet them. This experience was very exciting for the kids and made for some great pictures. The town had many shops and we had several very interesting conversations with the various shopkeepers. For instance, we learned what a milliner was (a hat maker, among other things) and the occupation's importance in the society of the time.

After strolling through the town we rode a tractor cart to a small working farm. The farm had a couple of horses, chickens, and a small pig sty. This was another favorite for the kids. They loved watching the little piglets run around in the pen. We all took a collective gasp of air when the daddy pig sat on his little ones. This annoyed the little piglets, but shortly after they settled into cuddling with dad once again.

On a later trip, we headed to Colonial Williamsburg after spending a day in Washington D.C. This is the largest living history museum in Virginia. The house tours were the best part of the visit. We were taken on a tour of each house while a period actor recounted the history of its former owners. We had lunch at one of the nicer restaurants in the town. We had to wait about an hour for a table, so we strolled around the shops and learned about wig-making, book-binding and silversmithing.

At the "olde" tavern, the food and atmosphere are definitely worth the wait. However, you do have the option to make reservations ahead of time by calling the restaurant. This is a good idea if you are on a tight schedule or just do not want to wait for a table. At the tavern, several period actors make their way from table to table with some thick period accents to bring some added merriment to your meal.

On still another trip, we visited an excellent museum in Boston, Massachusetts. When you go to the Boston Tea Party museum, you are invited to join a rally where you are given a brief history lesson about why the Boston Tea Party took place. Each audience member is given a card with the name and background of one of the Boston Tea Party participants and audience participation is encouraged.

After the rally, the group is led onto a small ship, where everyone gets a chance to toss their own crate of tea overboard. The museum itself has wonderful multimedia exhibits and the tour includes a chance to glimpse one of the original crates which held some tea leaves actually thrown overboard that fateful day. When visiting, take the time and go to Abigail's Tea Room. The tea and pastries are delicious and you get to keep the commemorative tea mugs.

On our second cross-country journey, we booked a room at the Excalibur hotel in Las Vegas through Expedia. We were trying to find a kid-friendly show and found the Tournament of Kings. This show is very much like the shows offered at Medieval Times venues across the country, but with a Las Vegas flair.

Since there was no silverware back in Medieval Times, the meal is meant to be eaten without it. This is lots of fun for kids who like to eat with their hands. Make sure everyone washes their hands before entering the dining area. We brought our antibacterial wet wipes along and shared them with some of the other guests.

When traveling through Connecticut in late May, we found a wonderful Revolutionary War reenactment. This annual event takes place on the Webb-Dean-Stevens museum grounds in Wethersfield, Connecticut. The museum itself offers delightful one-hour tours of magnificent mid-18th and early-19th century homes. The annual reenactment revolves around the Fifth Connecticut Regiment and the full-day reenactors are superbly knowledgeable. They are all dressed in full colonial costumes, cook on open fires around the encampments, and demonstrate marching and musket firing.

The kids were recruited into the regiment and got a chance to march and fire their own (wooden replica) muskets as well. Later, the kids got a chance to spend time with the field medic and learned in detail about 18th century field surgery and medicine. Most memorably, we learned about how smallpox inoculations were conducted during the time period; pretty disgusting, but effective and a significant help to the war effort.

We toured the historical houses and tried some of the authentic 18th century pastries sold in an open-air stall. Later in the day, we watched a battle re-enactment. It was amazing to see how slowly battles were actually conducted in those days, given proper rules of engagement and inaccurate firearms. It was much like choreographed dance, but perilous to be sure.

On our way home from our trip to Seattle, we decided to stop at an additional, unplanned attraction. **We looked through some pamphlets that we found displayed in the lobby of our hotel.** This is a great way to find out about the offerings in any area you stop for the night. Most hotel lobbies have displays filled with pamphlets from local businesses and attractions. Some of these pamphlets even include discount coupons.

We were in Fort Wayne, Indiana and found two attractions we thought would be fun. The first was a store/factory for DeBrand fine chocolates. We stopped in the little shop, got a chance to sample some excellent chocolate, shared a few scoops of ice cream, and purchased some gift assortments for friends and family back home.

The local time-travel attraction was the historic Fort Wayne. That weekend happened to be one of the reenactment weekends at the Fort. For a few dollars, we were invited to walk around and learn about the struggle that took place there during the French-Indian War in 1791. Here, as in our experience in Connecticut, we found the reenactors knowledgeable, friendly and quite serious about their roles.

We walked into the apothecary and got an in-depth lesson about the medical offerings of the time. The young chemist who sat in the apothecary shop was entertaining and great with our kids. The Fort Wayne reenactors spend the weekend at the Fort. We met whole families that took part in the event, including young, adorable children running around in period clothing. This is a great family experience. Make sure to visit on a reenactment weekend.

Getting Your Family on the Road/ Getting the Kids Involved

1. On the road as a family, learning as a family is one of the most enjoyable experiences. Look for opportunities for

the kids to do some research too as you plan stops that explore the space program and time-travel destinations and events.

2. Use VisitNasa.com to see which N.A.S.A. destinations may be convenient to include in your travel route. This is most helpful when traveling the southern corridor from Texas to Florida.

3. At N.A.S.A. destinations, always take the bus tour. This is likely to be the most amazing and memorable experience of the visit. Budget at least three hours per N.A.S.A. stop so you have time for the shuttle tour experience.

4. Encourage your kids (and each other) to take part in the unique experiences of these destinations. Whether it is meeting a real-life astronaut or asking a few questions of that 19th century milliner, these will be some of the most memorable moments of your road trip.

5. Time-travel destinations are a wonderful way of involving the kids (and yourselves) in a four-dimensional world of the past. Do some advance research if possible and take a few guided tours to start your visit, if available. These measures will orient you to your new surroundings and jump-start your enjoyment.

6. Search the internet ahead of time to find out what time-travel events may coincide with your travel dates or find great events to plan travel around.

7. Reenactors at time-travel destinations are almost always friendly, informed and eager to impart their knowledge. Have fun talking with them and encourage the kids to ask all their questions.

8. With both space and time-travel destinations, there may be a lot to absorb for both the adults and the kids. After visits, it is a good idea to recap the attraction and each choose favorite parts in order to weave together the narrative you will take away as a family.

9. Some space and time-travel events are rather expensive, but especially memorable. Within the confines of your family budget, choose a few events you are all especially excited about.

10. Wherever you are headed, there is likely some time-travel or space-related experience on your route. Just go and enjoy galactic wonder or go backward in historical whimsy!

Chapter 11

Ride with Us: Our 15 Trips Under 1 Week

"I have found that there ain't no surer way to find out whether you like people or hate them than to travel with them."

— *Mark Twain, Tom Sawyer Abroad*

OUR FAMILY STARTED OUT with a goal: to reach all states accessible by car by the time our kids went off to college. We thought it would be wonderful bonding time and we were right. We also thought it would take at least a decade and we were wrong; getting to 49 states took less than 3 years. As each trip built on the previous one, we found we were making incredible time on our quest, hoarding vacation time at work while working around the kids' school schedules. We began to explore further every chance we could.

In order to enjoy your own family road tripping, you may need a place to start. We offer the trip routes we have taken as this potential starting point. Your own geography will make a difference here as you consider your first few trips. From our New Jersey home, the time allotted to each journey was highly condensed. The momentum of our travels carried us forward. Pick your own pace, pick your first few trip destinations and make a few of the stops we recommend from experience along the way.

In general, there are really two types of trips we have taken: shorter trips which have been most common and three longer, cross-country trips which we will detail later. **We recommend starting with shorter trips**, especially with kids in tow. Below are the 15 trips that each took between half a day and five days. Remember to use your geography to your advantage: even when your goal is to explore the whole country, **there are wonderful destinations close to home**.

1. NEW HAMPSHIRE, MAINE AND VERMONT
(April 2014)—3 days

This was our first trip once our goal had been set and really was ambitious at the time. Every one of these states was new to all four of us and, though close to home, this was further than we had ever ventured by car as a family.

We found a wonderful recitation of Dr. Seuss' *Lorax*, which included a free pancake breakfast sponsored by the local chamber of commerce in Intervale, New Hampshire. We then explored the Weather Discovery Center in North Conway, New

Hampshire. The Weather Discovery Center has great exhibits for kids including many interactive stations. Next to the museum, there is a main street full of shops to browse during a brief stroll as well.

In the evening, we took a trip to Winslow, Maine where our hotel had recommended we visit the Lobster Trap & Steakhouse for a lobster dinner. We knew two things about Maine going into this trip—the fictional "Cabot Cove" from *Murder She Wrote* might be an attraction lead (it turned out we did not find success with this lead) and lobster was the famed delicacy. We certainly enjoyed our dinner and we all wore our lobster bibs for good measure and for a few pictures.

We ended up making the most stops in Vermont to explore destinations with wine, cheese, maple syrup, chocolate, ice cream, and teddy bears. The most family-friendly and memorable of these was the Ben & Jerry's factory in Waterbury. We took a wonderful tour of the factory with a very entertaining guide. There is much fun to be had and the most fun stop for us and the kids was the Flavor Graveyard. It is not scary and you will even find yourselves laughing graveside. The cutest stop, loved by the kids, was the Vermont Teddy Bear factory in Burlington, complete with lots of Bear Wear (clothing) and a Bear Hospital.

2. CONNECTICUT, MASSACHUSETTS AND RHODE ISLAND (May 2014)—3 days

The first trip had motivated us to continue on, so a month later we were on the road again. Having enjoyed the *Lorax* event in the previous trip, we were anxious to find another "event" type attraction and found a great Revolutionary War period reenactment in Westfield, Connecticut. The war reenactment itself was fun to watch and the kids even got to practice marching in formation while toting wooden pieces shaped like muskets.

The best part of this annual event, however, are the tents where you can explore the crafts, medicines, clothes, and other items that were available and marketed in the time period. There is an authentic feel and enthusiasm among the vendors that makes the event a lot of fun, especially for the kids.

In Massachusetts, we focused on Boston itself and visited the Boston Tea Party Ships and Museum. There is a rousing town meeting to be a part of and, of course, you can toss some "tea crates" into the Fort Point Channel to feel the civil disobedience in your bones. We stopped by the *Cheers* pub as well to meet a friend for lunch. Ben completed his first eating contest by polishing off the "Norm Burger" which merited an honorable mention on the official CheersBoston.com website; his accolade is still on display there!

In Providence, Rhode Island, we visited the annual WaterFire event at the River Walk in the evening. It is beautiful to see the small camp fires dotting the river while walking the downtown as a family. There are also plenty of music and food options as you stroll the city. The weather, even at this time of year, can be chilly, so bring jackets for the nighttime event.

3. DELAWARE
(June 2014)—1 day

We drove down to Delaware City and took the ferry to Fort Delaware on Pea Patch Island. The Fort was perhaps most famously a Union prison for Confederate soldiers captured in the Civil War. The ferry itself is an experience and the Fort is a trip back in time with reenactment shows that are fun for kids and adults as you observe 1800s customs.

Our favorite program during the visit was watching a play of two ladies taking afternoon tea in the middle of the central courtyard. This play gave us a brief glimpse into a day in the life of the Fort. Another favorite aspect was the live blacksmith demonstration. It was fascinating to watch the blacksmith forge an iron hook using only the tools from the era. We also walked through the rooms of the Fort with decor and amenities of the 1800s.

4. MARYLAND, NORTH CAROLINA, SOUTH CAROLINA, GEORGIA AND FLORIDA
(June 2014)—3 days

This was our first real extreme family road trip because of the short timeframe and large distance to cover. There were 30 hours of driving with a full day of walking in the middle. This trip centered around our first Disney park with the kids, the Magic Kingdom. It was absolutely as magical as the name suggests, a great entree into the pixie-dust filled world of Walt Disney.

We decided to make this particular destination a surprise for the kids and this added to our parental excitement from the initial stages of planning until arrival. The kids did not know where we were going until we pointed out the signs proclaiming that Disney World was coming up at our next exit. We made some quick stops and saw some cities by car in the other states to and from Florida. A particularly memorable stop was a delicious crab lunch at Woody's Crab House in North East, Maryland. This touristy restaurant is an attraction in itself.

5. PENNSYLVANIA, WEST VIRGINIA AND OHIO (September 2014)—2 days

After the 2014 Fantasy Football draft, we decided it was time to visit the Football Hall of Fame in Canton, Ohio. We left the house on the evening of the draft, drove as far as we could and slept in Pittsburg, Pennsylvania. We visited the National Aviary there for a few hours the next morning before heading to Canton.

The Football Hall of Fame is a wonderful museum of history and memorabilia, but the highlight is the "Super Bowl Experience" at the top. This Experience is a blow-by-blow highlight reel of the previous Super Bowl in surround-sound immersion.

On the way back, we drove through downtown Wheeling, West Virginia and stopped at our first Cheddar's restaurant. This is a great, reasonably-priced, family restaurant chain. We particularly enjoyed the giant warm chocolate chip cookie and ice cream desert.

6. NEW JERSEY
(November 2014)—1 day

The kids were off school for a day and we decided to take a day trip in-state to visit Liberty Science Center about two hours away in Jersey City. This is a superb science museum with exhibits, IMAX movies and all you would expect from a top-notch science center appealing to kids.

A unique aspect of our visit, however, was the Virus Laboratory where the kids tested simulated blood samples to see which was infected. The kids donned lab coats and goggles and it was wonderful to watch them use droppers, test tubes and microscopes in their pursuit of scientific truths.

On the way to the museum, we glimpsed the Statue of Liberty and, instinctively, stopped to the car to take a few quick pictures. Though we considered including the Statue in that day trip, time would not allow us to see both the Museum and Statue. We opted for our original plan, but vowed to return to the green beacon of liberty in the near future.

7. MISSISSIPPI, LOUISIANA, ALABAMA AND TENNESSEE
(November 2014)—4 days

For this trip, we decided we needed to discover some more of the South. We parents had been to New Orleans before, but wanted to take the kids. Other than Louisiana, these were new states for all of us.

N.A.S.A. attractions in Mississippi (Stennis in Hancock County) and Alabama (U.S. Space and Rocket Center in Huntsville) are amazing, particularly the base bus tours. In between, we went to New Orleans, strolled the French quarter, enjoyed some beignets and had a tasty lunch right on Canal Street.

Being close by, we wanted to get to a sight in Tennessee, so we travelled there on the way back. We ended up seeing the Parthenon in Nashville all lit up in vibrant, rainbow colors at night. It was beautiful to behold, though mostly abandoned on the evening we went there. Once we realized we were alone and after snapping a few pictures, we power-walked back to the car.

8. NEW YORK
(December 2014)—1 day

After seeing the Statue of Liberty from afar, we travelled back to see the giant monument a month later. The Statue of Liberty island is bigger than it looks from afar and we walked all around, enjoying some snacks and bird watching as we went. We each got a headset with a personalized listening tour before heading closer to Lady Liberty. The listening tours are tailored for adults or children and give some context and quick history of the monument.

We also explored Ellis Island and the ferry ride, an attraction in itself with a nice view of New York City. As part of the Ellis Island experience, Ben looked up his grandmother's mother's record traveling from Russia through Ellis Island in the 1910s. We were delighted to find a certificate that included her name, age and declared occupation at the time she arrived at Ellis Island.

9. TENNESSEE, ARKANSAS, TEXAS, OKLAHOMA, KANSAS, MISSOURI AND ILLINOIS
(May 2015)—5 days

This time, we went further into Tennessee, to Memphis, and our stop was Graceland. It is a must-see attraction and well-kept with lots of memorabilia, many cars and much history (even Elvis' grave). With kids, though, you have to keep your party moving despite all there is to see. Graceland offers an option of a personalized electronic tour using iPads. The kids loved holding their own electronics and listening to the tour with the attached headsets. At the end of the tour, there is a great photo opportunity in front of the main house. This is a picturesque site and a great backdrop for your family photo.

We drove through downtown Little Rock, Arkansas and took in some sights by car en route to Dallas, Texas where we stayed at a *Dallas* television show-themed hotel. Pictures of the television cast line the hallways of this hotel and if you book the rooms early enough, you can stay at the Miss Ellie or J.R. suites. The next day, we visited the *Dallas* show mansion set and grounds. The guided tour is a must and the mansion and grounds are well-kept and fun to explore.

Heading north to Oklahoma City, we visited the Cowboy Museum. The museum offers a robust experience while describing the history of cowboy life . We arrived on the weekend of the annual Chuck Wagon gathering at the museum. This included pony rides outside and arts and crafts for the kids inside. The kids even got a chance to sit on a real, and very large, bull. There are beautiful paintings and movies worth watching. For our next stop in Wichita, Kansas, we had superb barbeque and took a few family photos with the picturesque Keeper of the Plains statue.

We kept moving north to Missouri where we visited the Mark Twain Museum and town in Hannibal. We walked a terrific 2 hour tour between buildings in a village atmosphere. These buildings include Mark Twain's family home as well as the homes of the friends on whom he based the characters of Huck Finn and Becky Thatcher. Of course, the storied white picket fence is there to be painted (or at least there for a photo op that looks like you are painting). Across the street, you can sample some of Missouri's state dessert: ice cream.

Perhaps our biggest surprise find on this trip was the Lincoln Library in Springfield, Illinois. We did not know what to expect, but the Library's exhibits absolutely came alive and enthralled us. The mannequins they use to tell Lincoln's stories are quite life-like. We took many excellent pictures with them.

10. WISCONSIN, ILLINOIS AND MICHIGAN
(July 2015)—3 days

This trip was well-planned with three stops and no detours. We began with the Jelly Belly Factory in Pleasant Prairie, Wisconsin. It is really a warehouse with a carefully-orchestrated "factory tour" devoted to those delicious jelly beans. We got some free samples at the end of the tour which lets out at the gift shop and stopped at the sample bar to try a few new flavors. After picking out a few assortments of jelly beans to take home, we headed for our next attraction.

With that quick visit behind us, we set our navigation to Chicago and did an impromptu walking tour there. The sight we were most excited about was the giant, reflective Bean. It seems we were working on a "bean" theme to this trip. We took many pictures from many angles at Chicago's famous, silvery monument. We then had some Chicago pizza and walked for about 3 miles through the attractive and clean city, particularly enjoying a few parks and the views of Lake Michigan.

The next day, we explored the Ford Museum in Dearborn, Michigan. It is an amazing collection of Americana and we particularly enjoyed the "Road Trip America" exhibit that was showing at the time. Go figure.

11. FLORIDA
(March 2016)—4 days

We were excited to go back to Florida to see the Kennedy Space Center and another Disney Park. Having been to Stennis and Huntsville facilities, we were keen to see another N.A.S.A. site. This was the largest and most impressive museum of the three, especially with the Space Shuttle Atlantis suspended in mid-air. The tour was amazing and we got to see a few real rocket-launching pads. The day we were there, there was even a SpaceX launch (SpaceX is a private spacecraft and rocket company). The rocket they were testing was successful going up, but did not stick the landing that particular day.

In the evening, we visited the famous Disney Polynesian dinner luau (we had gotten the meal plan that would cover this delicious outing). Ben had gone there as a child and it was as magical as he remembered. Even after a long day, we all had a delightful time, a great meal and enjoyed the dancing, singing and fire twirling.

We chose Epcot as our Disney park destination which was Mom and Dad's favorite park when they were young. It lived up to its lofty reputation and we saw nearly all the attractions in a single day including our favorite quadrant, the World Showcase. We got to really savor eating and exploring around all 11 countries included in the Showcase. This trip did not add a new state to our oversized pin-map at home, but was a wonderful collection of new experiences.

12. QUEBEC
(March 2016)—2 days

This was our only international driving trip of the period. While we had not intended to take another trip so quickly, we were time-pressed to visit the famous Quebec Ice Hotel on its last open weekend of the season. The Ice Hotel was magnificent with carefully-designed rooms and common areas made of massive ice and packed snow. The lunch included in our tickets was a unique, regional culinary experience.

That night, we went to the elevated old city of Quebec City and walked the grounds to and from an authentic French meal. Immersed in the Canadian province of Quebec, Ben was speaking French on behalf of the family. It was like being in Europe, but we had gotten to our first stop in about 9 hours from home by car.

The next day, we explored the Olympic Park in Montreal. There are several attractions there and it is worthwhile to buy a combination ticket. We visited the inclined tower, the biodome and the planetarium. All were superb and family-friendly.

13. WASHINGTON D.C. AND VIRGINIA
(May 2016)—3 days

We walked over 10 miles in Washington D.C. staring with a Congressionally-acquired East Wing tour of the White House. To obtain these, you have to ask your Congressman, usually via internet, for tickets at least one month ahead. We then walked to the Lincoln Memorial and Washington Monument, walking next to the reflection pool and through the World War II, Korean and Vietnam Memorials. Next, we visited three Smithsonian museums: American History, Natural History and Native American.

The next day, we explored Colonial Williamsburg and walked another 5 miles or so. It was delightful time travel with shops, restaurants and people of the Colonial period. We began our tour at the Governor's Mansion which put the entire experience into its rightful context.

The following day we explored the International Spy Museum in Washington D.C. which was intriguing for the whole family. We learned that spy craft has quite a long, global history and you get to see many gadgets which are part of that rich history. Rosa's favorite memory was getting her picture taken with James Bond's Aston Martin within the temporary exhibit of James Bond villains throughout the years. The scavenger hunt is great for both kids and adults, ask for a free book when you purchase your tickets. We also all got to embrace a covert identity for the duration of our tour.

14. PENNSYLVANIA AND MICHIGAN
(July 2016)—2 days

We made an impromptu stop at Hershey's Chocolate World. Kids and adults enjoyed the free ride and chocolate samples. We then took about 20 minutes to browse some of the shops.

Afterword, we drove overnight to canoe on the western coast of Michigan and explored the Nelis Dutch Village in Holland, Michigan. The canoeing was a relaxing two hours and we spent close to three hours in the Dutch village. At the village, we each tried on wooden shoes and attended a lecture that described the process of making them.

We then headed home. This was the only multi-day trip where we did not stop at a hotel or motel to rest. Needless to say, we made incredible time.

15. NORTH CAROLINA, SOUTH CAROLINA, GEORGIA AND FLORIDA
(December 2016)—5 days

Before the trip, we felt we had previously only "driven through" the first three states above. On this trip we savored an experience in two states on the way to Universal Studios in Orlando, Florida. In Asheville, North Carolina, we spent an hour and a half at the Holiday Lights display in the North Carolina Arboretum. We also enjoyed the giant animatronic insect exhibit and the constellation keychain craft project there.

In Atlanta, Georgia, we took a self-guided tour of the World of Coca-Cola complete with polar bear picture, 4D movie and giant tasting room with 150 different flavors from around the world. Unfortunately, the guided tour was already sold out when we arrived at 9 a.m. for opening. Before we went into the museum, we posed for a few family photos with oversized Coke-themed sculptures in the adjacent park.

The Pirate Adventure dinner theater in Orlando was a great mix of adventure and humor, of theater and acrobatics. The next day, Universal Orlando was an amazing movie-magic experience (including Ben dancing with Minions in the street and taking part in the Animal Actors show). It turned out we had arrived during the busiest week of the year. This meant our attraction lines went up to 2 hours. We nonetheless persevered and saw all the attractions we wanted to during our 14-hour park day there. If at all possible, avoid the last week of December at theme parks.

In South Carolina, we visited the 500+ year old Angel Oak tree outside of Charleston and, after a restful hotel day, journeyed on to King's Mountain (a great, historic, Revolutionary War site) where the kids earned Junior Ranger badges yet again. There is a fun 2-mile hike as part of the exploration there which includes a visit to the Washington Monument replica (it is a lot smaller).

Chapter 12

Ride with Us: Our 3 Cross-Country Trips

"Our battered suitcases were piled on the sidewalk again; we had longer ways to go. But no matter, the road is life."

— *Jack Kerouac, On the Road*

W E SAVED UP OUR VACATION time and realized we could piggy back on some holidays and weekends to stretch these precious days even further. At this point, we had developed methods to enjoy shorter trips. We came to the realization we could travel cross-country in two big pushes to finish out our 48-state trek. We would drive further, and longer, and we would see the balance of the country together.

These cross-country trips were meant in some ways to push our limits, but we felt adventurous and emboldened by earlier successes. The longer voyages took more planning and more intentionality than the shorter road trips. We would have to choose a single stop in most states and we would have to follow the major roads more closely to voyage 7,000 miles or so in 9 to 11 days.

Originally, we were sure we could get to 48 states in two trips. We would then likely fly to Alaska and Hawaii at some later date. The road had other plans for us, however. After a most successful trip to the Northwest, the Southwest in December left us somewhat defeated.

In the Southwestern trip, we rerouted several times and missed several planned stops due to a combination of wind, snow and closed roads. We knew we needed to redo that particular trip and decided to add Alaska to the route the second time around. Alaska was set to be the most valuable pin in our map to date. After researching travel options, we found the least expensive and most practical way to reach Alaska: we would drive to the west coast and fly to Juneau and back from Los Angeles International Airport with a Seattle stopover each way.

A last general note. It is no accident our longest voyages happened in August and December. These are the times where the kids are off school and longer parental vacation time is easiest to take from work (at least in our particular workplaces). We planned the following trips for months, knowing the timing would be very tight. We knew these would be the most ambitious road trips and they each lived up to this designation. They were also the most immersive and awe-inspiring, the stuff that family legends are made of.

---

1. IOWA, NEBRASKA, SOUTH DAKOTA, WYOMING, OREGON, WASHINGTON, IDAHO, MONTANA, NORTH DAKOTA, MINNESOTA, WISCONSIN AND INDIANA
(August 2015)—9 days

We selected to travel the Northwest route first because we would leave the Southwest route for December's school break. We figured it would be harder to manage the northern cross-country route in winter months. We also thought the southern route would be better to take in the winter to avoid the summer heat. This thinking was ill-informed because of our lack of experience in the region. Apparently, even New Mexico sees its fair share of snow in the winter.

Our first stop was Living History Farms in Urbandale, Iowa. This was a fun stop with different time periods to explore as part of Iowa's cultural heritage. The kids most liked the wagon rides between farm sites and the various livestock and other farm animals we saw all around.

Next was Nebraska. We debated a few destinations and finally agreed on Scott's Bluff in Gering. It is there we learned about the Oregon Trail and, perhaps more importantly, about Junior Ranger books and activities. This was the site of the kids' first swearing-in ceremony as Junior Rangers.

In South Dakota, we went to the stop we had most wanted to see when embarking on this particular journey, Mount Rushmore, and its nearby, privately-funded cousin, Crazy Horse Memorial. These are two fantastic monuments. Mount Rushmore is epic and beautiful. Even though you know what you will be seeing, observing the gigantic set of presidents carved in stone is continually amazing as you walk the trails of the park and learn about how the monument was prepared over many years.

Crazy Horse is a different story about one family's multi-generational determination to build a Native American statue of pride over many, many decades. To give some perspective on the undertaking, after more than 60 years, the Crazy Horse monument is about 20% complete. We explored the museum and gift shop and most memorably, we enjoyed the spectacular, musical, laser light show projected on the unfinished monument from the comfort our car.

Wyoming was wonderful. We first made an unplanned stop just short of Yellowstone to ride horses in Cody. Each of us got our own horse and we rode for about an hour through the mountains and next to a rushing, turquoise river with eagles flying above. It was the first time the kids got to enjoy horseback riding in open nature.

We then continued to Yellowstone which is still one of our favorite National Parks. What is amazing about Yellowstone is it is a gigantic and beautiful park atop a live volcano. This creates many natural wonders including Old Faithful, geysers and thermal pools (all both interesting and stunning to observe).

In Oregon, we made a planned stop at the Four Rivers Cultural Center in Ontario. This is a very well-maintained museum, detailing five cultures that have called this particular region home and the heritage each people have brought with them. On the way from the Cultural Center to Washington State, we saw a billboard for the Geiser Grand Hotel. What made this billboard notable was that it was advertising an attraction more than 100 miles away. There must be something remarkable there, we thought.

The Hotel did not disappoint. We had a fantastic dinner in the main dining room, restored to its 1889 opening splendor. The dining room almost looks like a luxury cruise ship might have looked during the period with high ceilings, several floors within view above and ornate stained glass works. We especially enjoyed the wedge salad whose blue cheese recipe is authentic to 1889. Knowing this historical tidbit in advance makes the salad even more delicious.

In Washington, we visited the Twin Peaks diner right outside of Seattle for breakfast and then ventured into the City to enjoy lunch at the Space Needle. Lunch was a great experience for the kids as the revolving dining room spins ever so slowly during the meal. They get new views each time they look out and are able to pass notes to other tables without even leaving their seats by sticking them to the windows. The server provides post-it notes for just this reason. There are also various things to see from above on the observation platform, including giant spider sculptures on one nearby building roof top, and a smashed guitar on another.

In Idaho, we made a quick, 30-minute stop at the Potato Museum in Blackfoot, home of the largest potato crisp ever made. Then we were on our way to Little Bighorn (Custer's Last Stand) in Crow Agency, Montana. There is a sadness to this particular National Monument. In its own way, it marks the end of a certain period of Native American life on the continent. That said, it is the must-see attraction of the state and commemorates a unique moment in United States history. Just not a happy one.

In North Dakota, we stopped at the National Buffalo Museum in Jamestown and enjoyed seeing free-range buffalo from the museum's overlook. We especially enjoyed spotting White Cloud, the famed white buffalo and storied bringer of good tidings. Next door, we got to feed a family of buffalo.

We were off to Minnesota to visit the Eagle Preserve (this was a lovely chance to get up close to live eagles in the museum area and to spot wild eagles from several telescopes) in Wabasha the next day. En route, we made three unplanned stops that really make the state stand out in our memories.

First, we stopped at the "largest ball of twine" in Darwin, Minnesota. We got there after-hours so the adjacent museum was closed. We did get a chance, however, to read the ball's history and take a few pictures in front of the large, glass-encased gazebo that houses the twine ball 30 years in the making.

Further on the road, we were pretty hungry when we were passing the Mall of America in Bloomington. We figured we could stop for dinner, but on the way through we saw the indoor amusement park. We bought tickets for the rides and spent the next 75 minutes until the mall closed zooming up, down and around the amusement park, literally running from one ride to the next. It was incredible. We had such a great time we forgot we had stopped at the mall for dinner.

We reached our hotel in Wabasha late that night. We booked a suite in the AmericInn hotel there. The suite had a room for the kids with a pull out sofa and a flat screen TV. Our room had a king size bed, fireplace and hot tub. This was one of our favorite hotel stays among all of our trips. The hotel itself is decorated with posters and images of the movies *Grumpy Old Men* and *Grumpier Old Men*. Both were filmed in Wabasha.

On a recommendation from a friend, we went to see the House on the Rock in Spring Green, Wisconsin. The attraction is pretty amazing, but macabre as well. The house is actually built into the earth, with trees and rock protruding into the living areas and waterfalls running down walls. There are little stone creatures everywhere and instruments that are playing on their own. There are also picturesque marvels like the Infinity room and Japanese garden area.

The House is worth seeing, but take note of the ominous, dark-looking elements throughout when traveling with kids at your side. This is probably not an appropriate stop for very little ones. While touring the house, we noticed visitors carrying small boxes with multicolored fudge. We stopped at the gift shop and, after sampling some, bought a box of our own. It was some of the best fudge we have ever tasted.

On the way home, we stopped at Fort Wayne, Indiana for the night and found there was a Fort reenactment the next day. This was fun time-travel and we learned about Fort history. The reenactors themselves had children with them too. Evidently, the Fort Wayne reenactment weekends are a family affair.

2. Missouri, New Mexico, Arizona, Nevada, California, Utah and Colorado
(December 2015)—11 days

This was an exciting trip at the start. We would reach several new states to get to 48 total and had not faced much adversity until this point. That last part was all about to change. It just did not occur to us that traveling the American Southwest in December would be a problem. And it was.

Our first stop was the Gateway Arch in Saint Louis, Missouri. We had all wanted to visit the structure, having passed by it before. There is also a nearby courthouse museum that is ornate and has an interesting exhibit on Frederick Douglas. The Arch itself is a fun trip up in a train car of sorts and once you are at the top, there are great views of Saint Louis through tinier windows than you would imagine. You get a good look at two sports stadiums among other local landmarks.

Driving through Colorado, we experienced so much "winter wonderland" and closed "passes" that we rerouted to Roswell, New Mexico. The UFO museum there is well-done, but 45 minutes is all you need to explore it fully. We then caught only the tail end of a horrific snow storm as we left New Mexico en route to Arizona.

Of all of our grand plans for Arizona (including the "grandest" of canyons), we only managed to see the Petrified Forest/Painted Desert (these are the same National Park, connected to each other) which was beautiful to behold as we approached sunset. We got there late in the day and Park staff informed us we could not stop the car. We could only drive through the Park or risk a Park ticket. That is what we did. Really. Any photographs to the contrary are in error.

We took an hour to explore the Hoover Dam in Nevada the next day and continued on to Las Vegas. In all seriousness, this was a wonderful, bright spot in the trip. Vegas is great fun for kids, you just need to judge quickly what to explore and what to avoid. In our three-hour walking tour of the bright-light city, we saw about a dozen mascot characters including SpongeBob and Mickey Mouse. We also saw the magnificent, free Bellagio dancing water show. We walked in and out of Vegas hotels that are wonderfully ornate and impeccably themed. That evening, we had purchased tickets to the Tournament of Kings Holiday Show playing at our hotel, Excalibur. It was exceptionally entertaining, a Vegas-level "Medieval Times" experience.

We visited with two friends in Los Angeles and our cousins in Santa Cruz the next day. Insisting we needed an "attraction" to mark California, we took a whole bunch of family pictures in front of the Giant Thermometer in Baker, California. We ended up missing Yosemite (due to snow) and the Grand Canyon (due to timing) on this trip and, by this time, scratched out a few other attractions. The mounds of snow and ice in the region had humbled us.

We did opt to stop by Las Vegas again on the way back home from California because the city had so picked up our spirits the first time through. We spent some time in the Venetian enjoying lobster skewers, the promenade of shops under the painted sky and the gondolas passing by on the central canal. We even purchased a few jewelry pieces which included pearls fresh from the oysters.

Part of the charm of the oyster jewelry stands is the option to choose your own oyster. After the salesperson whispers a special chant over your oyster, you get to see what pearl is hiding inside. You have the option of just purchasing the pearl or adding a ring or pendant onto which to mount the pearl. The pearl itself is relatively inexpensive, but beware—the jewelry can be quite pricey. Ask the salesperson for a mounting piece within your budget.

Though a few national parks did get scratched from this trip itinerary (among them Bryce and Zion), we did choose to venture to Arches National Park in Utah. It was beautiful with snow-covered red rock and picturesque views for miles and miles. We drove through, stopping at several points to do some minor hiking and some major picture-taking.

We got to Mesa Verde National Park in Colorado much later than planned. We spent about one hour driving up icy hills in the dark only to find the final road to the cliff dwellings blocked. We had reached them after operating hours. We knew what we had to do: get back on the road and head to Denver, Colorado.

After breakfast in Denver the next morning, we headed home. Despite some setbacks, we had achieved our "lower 48" goal. But this last trip did not sit quite right with us parents between the terrible weather, frequent rerouting and missed stops. What would we do next and how would we "make it right?"

3. COLORADO, UTAH, CALIFORNIA, ALASKA, ARIZONA, NEW MEXICO AND KANSAS
(August 2016)—10 days

After many family conversations, this trip would be both a do-over of the previous cross-country trip and our first foray into air travel (to Juneau, Alaska), which would be most afford-able from Los Angeles International Airport, LAX. We had been encouraged and taunted on Twitter to get to the 49th state accessible by car. While we did not have the time to make the car journey straight to Alaska, we figured that a 7,000+ mile road trip to the other coast and back as part of the trip would put Alaska in the "road trip" achievement category.

Our chosen Alaskan city, Juneau, is actually not accessible by car at all since it is surrounded by an ice shelf on one side and an ocean on the other. We would have been sorely disappointed to have driven all the way to the ice shelf only to realize we had to turn back! We also had not been able to visit as many sights as planned on our last trek. We figured we would not repeat any attraction, but would go to the ones we had missed and add a few to the itinerary.

The first attraction stop, totally unplanned, was in Oakley, Kansas. We headed out from New Jersey knowing there was plenty of road ahead before we would truly begin our journey. This would be the furthest we had ever gone without some mid-way attraction stops. As it happened, about halfway through Kansas, we were watching beautiful lightning storms on the road. Though captivating, these storms were somewhat unnerv-ing and we searched for a place to stop once the lightning was behind us. We happened upon a humungous Buffalo Bill statue (with a huge buffalo statue beside it) in Oakley. This was a perfect spot for leg-stretching and dozens of family photos.

Next, a friend had recommended Great Sand Dunes National Park in Mosca, Colorado. There is sand-sledding there and, having experienced Colorado snow in winter, sand in summer seemed a better landscape. We loved this park and walked through shallow waters and porous sand to climb some tall sand dunes. Though others had rented sand sleds at the Visitor Center, we had unintentionally missed the opportunity. There was only one choice left: Ben and the kids threw themselves down the first set of sand dunes. There would be sand in our shoes the entire rest of the vacation, but it was worth it and made for some great action photos!

Next, we visited Mesa Verde, by daylight this time. It was incredible and we stopped at quite a few spots to observe the constructs of the native peoples as far back at 600 A.D. Though we did not take the close-up walking tour of the famous cliff dwellings, we did get quite a view and many fantastic pictures at one of the beautiful viewpoints along the way.

We missed Four Corners National Monument which was to be our next stop. Rosa had visited the monument years before and remembered it as being an open space with a small, raised platform that allowed you to stand in all four states at once. We came upon a gated attraction this time and the gates were locked since we got there after official visiting hours for the day had ended. In total, we have missed this same attraction four times in our family travels. We figure this one is just not meant to be—for now.

Bryce Canyon National Park in Utah was nothing short of breathtaking, beautiful, impressive and completely photogenic every step of the way. The first stop when you enter the park, Rainbow Point, is so amazing we spent our time there and used all our energy to hike down and then (much more slowly) up. The backdrop is miles of red rock and it goes deep so bring your hiking spirit and comfortable shoes. You are going down and then up about 25 stories and walking more than two miles total on the path we took. Keep in mind we did this with a 9 and a 7-year-old. Zion National Park was beautiful to behold, but we mostly drove through and stopped for a few pictures among the towering mountains.

Disneyland in Anaheim, California is smaller than Magic Kingdom in Florida with almost as much to see. That was good because we got to see our top 19 rides in only 9 hours. Much like in Florida, the trick was to use "fast passes." We loved the new Star Wars theme throughout Tomorrowland. Due to the sheer joy and excitement from the kids, our favorite ride was Autopia by Honda: each kid behind the wheel of their own car, driving a parent for a change of pace.

Juneau, Alaska was amazing. The Mendenhall Glacier was a sight to behold. It had a beautiful bluish quality to it against the backdrop of two mountains with a vast, pristine lake in front. We decided to take the 45 minute walk back and forth to Nugget Falls, another breathtaking sight. Later, on top of Mount Roberts after taking the tramway, there are marvelous views as the downtown becomes smaller and the incoming tides and outlying mountains become visible. On the mountain, we got to enjoy the culinary delight of fresh Alaskan salmon and the most delicious and ornate hot chocolate we have ever experienced. We also took the town trolley tour, 45 worthwhile minutes of history and local notes.

Once we arrived back in Los Angeles, we hit the road with adrenaline pumping, drove all night, and made it to the Grand Canyon in the early morning. We were just in time to watch the sun come up over the rocks. The Grand Canyon is incredible and the first stop, at the Visitor Center, gives you the best vista as you walk around for half a mile near the edge. The Canyon is a must-see attraction and quite a big park, so we made several stops to see one majestic overlook after another.

Aztec Ruins in New Mexico was our favorite "civilization" stop on the trip. We got to explore 3 kivas (holy houses) restored on site and to walk through many of the dwellings, going through short doorways and touching some 1,000-year-old rocks that have been restored nicely. We also enjoyed seeing the indigenous wildlife all around us.

It was time to hit the road again, all the way to the middle of Kansas. After a night's sleep, we found an attractive brochure and decided our last adventure on this trip would be the Land Of Oz Museum in Wamego, Kansas. The winery and taco shop are charming and the folks at both are very attentive and hospitable. The museum itself (complete with lots of memorabilia) is a fun, quick stop. It is full of life-sized mannequins of the main characters from the film that are great for kids and photo ops in scenes with Dorothy and her crew.

Chapter 13

Our Top Stops

"See the world. It's more fantastic than any dream
made or paid for in factories."

— *Ray Bradbury, Fahrenheit 451*

ALL OF OUR ROAD TRIPS have been unforgettable journeys into discovery and family bonding. Each trip has had its own aura, geography and unique family narrative. Starting with the planning stage, the excitement and anticipation for the journey fuels the adventure to come. The trips themselves have been full of wonder and new experiences. Every time we crossed a new state line and cheered as we passed the state's unique welcome sign, we knew we were going to discover a culture and environment found only in that particular part of the country. We love the changes in accents, attitudes, cuisines and scenery.

We have traveled more than 40,000 miles during our family road tripping adventures and have explored many diverse attractions and stops. Some of our destinations were researched at length before we started our trek and others were found along the way. We have all enjoyed the places we have seen and each of us has our favorites. We decided each of us would tell you, in our own words, about our favorite road trip destination. Narrowing the list down to a single top pick proved difficult, but ultimately we each chose a different highlight on which to focus.

ELLA (AGE 8)

You're probably wondering "how do these kids get through a road trip without fighting?" Well, it is easy when you are thinking about the amazing trip you are going to have. We have been on amazing trips these past years, but my favorite is when we went to breakfast with the Lorax in Intervale, New Hampshire.

Let's talk about the Lorax, my favorite stop. We had a wonderful pancake breakfast. To get in, we donated *Fox in Socks* (my personal favorite Dr. Seuss book). It was about Fox teaching Knox rhymes.

It was an adorable show they put on for us. It was the whole show of the Lorax. There is a furry something that claims his name is "the Lorax" and he protects Truffula trees. Someone chops down the trees and everyone moves away. At the end, a kid makes more Truffula trees.

There were treats related to the Lorax where they had cake pops that were Truffula trees. There were beautiful crafts and you could meet the Lorax, but it was over quickly.

On the nearby nature trail in the woods, I was wearing sneakers. It was slippery, cold and made my butt wet, but it was fun.

It was interesting how they took the sap out of the trees to make syrup. I recommend this for ages 3 and up.

Danny (age 10)

My favorite stop in all my trips was Coca-Cola World in Atlanta, Georgia. At home, one of my favorite drinks (when my parents let me have it) is Coke. But not for breakfast. And not at home most of the time.

I found out that Coca-Cola World existed in school when my teacher was talking about regions in the nation. When I discovered it was a possible stop on our trip to Florida, I was so excited to go. My Dad said I would prefer Universal Studios on that trip, but it did not turn out to be the case.

This World was one unique experience I will never forget. My favorite part by far is the tasting room. Just imagine 100+ flavors of Coke from all around the world in one giant room, but at the end of the day I love some Sprite. There is something, a soft drink called gingerbread Coke, which amazingly tastes really good.

Although the tasting room is epic, I still have tons more to talk about. There is a 4D movie about Coke which is awesome. In the movie, scientists were figuring out what makes Coca-Cola taste so special. This did not make sense to me because all you have to do is look at the ingredients. Meanwhile, we bounced around in our seats and got sprayed with air and water.

Another great thing about Coca-Cola World is there is a commercial room where you see lots of commercials. My favorite commercial was the one with Mean Joe Green. There was also the secret formula vault and I got to design my own Coke poster and email it to myself. Yes, I have my own email address. My sister and I also got to meet the Coke polar bear and take a picture with him. Those are my favorite places at Coca-Cola World. I highly recommend this stop on your road trip.

BEN

There are so many travel destinations that have been my favorites in different ways. "Favorite destination" is almost too hard a question to give a single answer. Thinking about it for a short while, however, I do most enjoy attractions that allow you to "tour the world" in a single location. The first location which comes to my mind is the 11-country tour in Epcot Center in Orlando, Florida (I loved it as a kid and even more as an adult showing my kids). Even more magnificent in our family road travels with the kids, however, was Las Vegas.

Sin City, with kids? Las Vegas is the perfect setting for a family road trip with kids for quite a few reasons. There is a tremendous amount of interesting walking to do and during your stroll you are likely to bump into a dozen people dressed as cute cartoon characters like SpongeBob or Elmo or Mickey Mouse. Mile for mile, you will encounter as many animated characters in Las Vegas as you would in Disneyland or Disney World. Plus, you rarely have a line for that great photo op with your kids and the beloved character of your choice for a tip of a few dollars (and remember, no park admission).

Las Vegas is a journey around the world *and* through time. Whether you are exploring the beauty of ancient Rome or modern-day Venice, you are immersed in a wonderful world full of window-shopping and gourmet food at the ready. For example, we enjoyed both fancy gelato and skewered lobster in Venice within 20 minutes at two different restaurants. A short distance away, we dined at a wonderful French café for breakfast the following day in Paris. In between, we enjoyed an excitingly themed show in Excalibur, the Tournament of Kings, taking us back to Medieval European times (complete with a finger-licking feast).

There are spectacular sights to see. We went all the way up the Eiffel Tower and got a magnificent view of the whole Las Vegas Strip. We also waited only a short while for the splendid Bellagio water show to dance around and light the night. We wandered through New York City streets and enjoyed a few restaurants as we each chose our own favorite foods and sat down on a nearby New York park bench to enjoy them all. We took at least a dozen photographs just in the ancient Egyptian Luxor and nearly one hundred photos during a three-hour walk of the bright-light city.

Of course, Las Vegas is not without its dangers and wrong turns. Beware of folks on street corners trying to give you pamphlets, the scores of panhandlers in your midst, and half-naked folks that are peddling the latest night club. The main attraction of the town is gambling and you will not enjoy this with little ones at your feet (plus that is not allowed by security personnel). The hotels/casinos may even seem "gaudy" or "fake" to you and if that is your impression it will rub off on your whole family.

But, you can bask in the lights, the sights and the shows. You can enjoy the furry characters and the perfectly-themed spaces. The excitement of Las Vegas will catch fire with your kids too and you can all enjoy the spectacle, the world travel and the time travel too. We certainly did.

ROSA

It is difficult to pinpoint a favorite place among the myriad of destinations we have experienced. They were all fantastic. After much thought, however, I have chosen Quebec City, Canada as my favorite of our explorations. When we entered French Canada in our little Honda, we were entering a brand new country. The man at the entry check point smiled as he looked at our passports and asked us where we were heading. When we gleefully told him we were going to see the Ice Hotel, he asked us if we had made a "rezzy" at the hotel. Even though he was speaking English, we stopped and had to take a moment to translate in our heads.

No, we did not have a reservation at the Ice Hotel. We would be staying at the Ambassador Hotel in Quebec City. The street signs changed from English to French and the speed limit signs from miles to kilometers per hour. We searched the Honda dashboard and instruction manual to find the button that would show us how many kilometers per hour we were traveling. We did not want to get a ticket in our first few minutes as guests in the Queen's realm.

Our first stop was Hotel De Glace (French for "Ice Hotel"). We would never have considered this stop if it were not for little Ella asking us to go here. What an unbelievable experience. The hotel itself was a long series of interconnected tunnels and rooms of varying sizes and shapes. The main hall had several bars carved out of ice, offering beverages in glasses made of ice.

This is such an environmentally friendly idea. The glasses keep the drink cold and then melt down when they are no longer needed. The beds are made of ice. Some are elaborately carved and others are simple and functional. Many of the rooms have wonderfully themed carvings in the walls and on the ice furniture. A number of the rooms and common areas have colorful lights to accentuate the ice carvings. The doors are all made of draped fabric, and the bathrooms are in an adjacent building.

This is not a hotel we would stay at, but it is wonderful to explore. We prefer warm, soft beds and indoor plumbing. We walked around the grounds and found two ice slides, a sauna and a few bubbling hot tubs surrounded by ice and snow. We each tried the ice slides and the four of us, together, experienced the sauna for a few minutes (even in our winter coats).

The entrance fee included a tasting menu of sorts. We entered the commissary and tried a variety of samples of local French Canadian cuisine. After lunch, we walked over to an outdoor bar made of snow. We were given wooden popsicle sticks and watched as molten maple syrup was poured onto the bar. We were instructed to roll the now hardening sticky treat onto our sticks and eat it. This was one of the best desserts I have ever had. The combination of the warm sweetness of the syrup and the frozen, textured snow results in a sensation unlike anything I have ever tasted. I think of this sense memory every time I remember the Ice Hotel.

Our next stop was the Ambassador Hotel. This hotel is lovely and inviting. The staff are friendly and accommodating, and the rooms clean and warm. My favorite aspect of this hotel is the indoor pool area which includes a heated pool, splash zone for the kids, hot tub, and several bird cages with colorful, delightful occupants.

We explored Quebec City that night. We took the funicular up to the Old City. The funicular is a glass elevator that goes up on a steep angle rather than straight up. It is something of a hybrid of an elevator and escalator. We found a small restaurant and tried more local French Canadian food.

Quebec City feels like a small, European town. The locals are happy to speak to you in either English or French, or a combination of the two. Our waitress spoke to Ben in French while she and I conversed in English. My high school French is not as good as Ben's and I am more comfortable answering in English, though I did understand a good portion of what was said in French. My high school French teacher would be proud. We walked around, breathed in the crisp air, and admired the old buildings, sculptures and small shops before heading back to our hotel for the night.

Of all our road trips, this relatively short trip into French Canada was my favorite. We were in an entirely different country with its own history, culture and currency (note they do accept U.S. dollars). Perhaps best of all, we were able to accomplish this international journey in the comfort of our family car.

Chapter 14

Kids' Perspectives

"There are no facts, only interpretations."
— *Friedrich Nietzsche*

SOMETIMES YOU ARE WATCHING a favorite movie or television series and laughing at all the key lines. Sometimes you have memorized all of the dialog or most of it anyway. You know when the characters are going to enter and exit, the plot curves, the quirky moments and you are enjoying all of the tidbits. Usually, you and your spouse have some of these entertainment experiences together, some shared favorites that are always good for a re-watch when Netflix does not have anything tantalizingly new for the evening. But what if your kids were watching this entertainment favorite with you and the room was moving at 65 miles per hour?

Sometimes on family road trips, we parents are enjoying, experiencing, even celebrating and the kids are just not "with us." They do not "get" why a certain attraction has merited a fifth stop (what's a vista and can we stay in the car for this one?) or why we are staying through the whole 30 minute movie to figure out the context of a perfectly nice, seemingly simple attraction (so 4 presidents' heads, right?). And sometimes, by the same token, the kids are enjoying something we would not consider that special or memorable (but we will be hearing about it for years to come).

We parents have begun to take note. On a family road trip with kids, those kids will have favorite activities, favorite quirky traditions, favorite foods, favorite sleep positions, favorite everything's for the entire journey. Many times, if you look through the eyes of your little voyagers, you will have quite a bit of fun seeing the travel through their vantage points. We asked our little people to tell us a bit about their perspectives in order to share with you.

Ella (age 8)

Some people think it is hard to travel by car. Well, it is actually not. I am not saying it is easy. Just it is not hard. Some mothers freak out thinking of the idea because they think it is dangerous. It is really not. For the parents it might seem scary, but to kids it is a dream come true. But soon your child will not want to travel with you. So do it before you cannot anymore.

You must pack audio books. Ask your kids what they want to listen to and if you want to pick some out you think they will like, read the back of the audio book to make sure this book is appropriate for your kids.

Kids are like birds. You have to let them fly away. So treasure the time you have together by going on a trip. You will bond, I guarantee. Every time you go you should always remember it is fun taking a trip alone, but with kids it is more memorable and you have the chance to talk.

For example, every day you pick up your kids from school and you ask "how was your day?" "Good" is not a good enough answer when you are in a car and have 1-8 hours left to your next destination. Otherwise, you will be bored for the rest of the 1-8-hour drive.

The more you talk to your kids, the more you will be able to know what is going on. For example, me and my brother thought we did not get along very well. So my Dad talked to us and found out we were fighting just because we were bored. So he turned on the radio and we listed to an audio book called *Middle School: The Worst Years of My Life* by James Patterson. Now enough about audio books, let us talk about games.

There are game options we have to do in the car. You can get travel games and give your kids electronics. The travel games are like games you play every day, only mini. Games like mini Monopoly, mini Clue and the card game version of Life. You can get a car table (you can probably spot it at Wal-Mart or Target). Make sure you have regular cards too! My personal favorite is picture time! It is where you see something awesome and you take a picture. It goes great for when I journalize.

Some small children might get homesick or start to cry, so you should pack a stuffed animal or bring a favorite object in the car. You can also pack a regular book to read to your child when you stop at a hotel to make them fall asleep.

Just in case you want to charge your phone on the road, get a travel charger and get a travel cord to go with it. Or, get a bunch of travel cords and chargers.

Every trip you get closer and closer. The more you travel, the more you will know what your kids like. That is the magic of the trip, bonding with your kids. Alright, that is all, but here are some easy tips on how to have fun on your trips:

1. Listen to your kids, what they have to say.
2. Let your kids look up what they want to see.
3. Make creative snacks and your kids' favorite snacks to bring on the trip.
4. Bring stuff for your kids to do.
5. Bring travel games.
6. Bring travel blankies and pillow pets.
7. Bring travel passports.
8. Play made up games.
9. Go to National Parks.
10. Do Junior Ranger programs, the kids get badges if they do it.
11. Stop at a rest stop to get more snacks.
12. When it is nighttime, check into a hotel.
13. Always pack paper bags.

14. With children under 3, do not keep small objects in the back seat.

15. Always wear seat belts.

16. Don't book a hotel at the last minute.

17. Don't play with markers in the car.

18. Watch pretty birds.

19. Do not bring pets.

20. Bring tooth brushes.

21. Don't pack small objects, they will get lost.

22. Pack appropriate audio books.

23. Ask your children what audio books they would like.

24. Choose a trip as a family.

25. When it is cold go south, when it is hot, go north.

26. Bring cards.

27. Bring small crafts.

28. Bring a coloring book.

29. Bring crayons.

30. Bring 2 bottles of water.

31. Buy a hot pot.

32. Buy a cooler.

33. Bring travel chargers and travel cords.

DANNY (AGE 10)

So, you have most likely heard about me in this book. Hello my name is Danny! I have a sister and a Dad and Mom. I am 10 years old (right now: check the date, I could be 40). I really like road tripping. I have been to 49 states (48 driving). In every car trip, I sit in the car. This is what that is like. I love to make pillow forts.

A difficulty in the car would be sleeping. That is why I bring many pillows. It is doubly hard when my sister is in the car, but here is the crazy thing: I have found ways to have plenty of sleep. You need to curl up and keep trying until you find a good spot. I am now an expert on "car sleeping." Here are some tips for a "sound night:"

1. Grab lots of pillows and blankets.
2. Find a foot rest.
3. Find a spot (this can take time).
4. Sleep.

Another nice thing in the car is entertainment. We have tried many things. I like board games and cards, but they are hard to play in the moving car. So, my absolute favorite activity is Mad Libs. The wacky, funny game is played on paper so it is easy to play in the car. Me and my sister make crazy stories. We still refer to our first one.

We discovered Mad Libs when my teacher gave me a copy. When we went to California to visit my cousins, they gave me and Ella some too. My sister and I were very happy and grateful. We played the whole way home.

Another great experience is swimming. Some motels and hotels have pools. As a result, we swim. My sister and I really like swimming. If you go on a road trip, you should pack a bathing suit. Here are some more ideas for your road trips:

1. Don't pack things that are not important. People will be cramped.
2. Pack a tooth brush.
3. Pack games like Monopoly, Clue and Connect 4.
4. Learn to sleep in the car.
5. Pack pillows.
6. Pack thick blankets. Don't pack sleeping bags.
7. Do attractions everyone might like.
8. Don't eat raw fish (sushi) in a land locked state. Long story.
9. Try new things.
10. Pack snack favorites like goldfish crackers and pretzels.
11. Mad Libs are fun, bring some with you.
12. Use at least 2 drivers.
13. Pack cards.
14. Bring a table to make sandwiches on. I like PB&J.
15. Bring some other types of foods: hot dogs, chicken fingers, hot chocolate, and cup of soup.
16. Audio books for kids are great to have.
17. Bring books such as *Big Nate*, *Diary of a Wimpy Kid*, and James Patterson books because they are the best and my favorite.
18. Pack activities like Word Searches, Crossword Puzzles and other Activity Books.
19. Get along with your sibling.
20. Bring chap stick.
21. Bring lots of clothes.

22. Keep track of time.

23. Take pictures.

24. Plan ahead.

25. Get plenty of sleep.

26. Always stop the car if someone needs to go to the bathroom.

Though we parents are still processing what these journal entries mean exactly, the clear theme seems to be that, for the kids, the journey is the experience rather than the stops along the way. Also, we have plenty of all-family bonding, but it seems our little ones are doing quite a bit of bonding with each other. We usually spend at least 10 hours per day in the car on a family road trip and they are usually keeping each other company while awake. Danny by his own estimation is a "car sleep expert" and Ella knows what it takes to make the car feel like bed at home.

After reading Danny and Ella's written thoughts and musings, we not only learn more about them, but are tickled to see the kids have picked up more than a few thoughts and ideas from us. It is great to know that Ella understands playing with markers in the car is inadvisable since they end up missing their cap and strewn all over our back seat along with colorful evidence. Danny has picked up the value of getting along with his little sister. Ella points out the importance of safety belts and keeping small objects away from young children. They both agree packing a toothbrush should be on everyone's check list.

Somewhere along the way, Ella realized the time we have to spend together as a family is fleeting. Danny feels that maybe we pack just a little too much into the back seat, which apparently leaves him feeling cramped. We love that both kids include the importance of taking pictures on a trip and making memories. That has always been one of our favorite activities on the road— making and recording experiences.

We are not quite sure why Ella thinks some mothers freak out worrying about the dangers on the road, but love that, to her, the road trip is a dream come true. Danny's comment about avoiding raw sushi in a land locked state is excellent advice that should not be taken lightly (do not ask, it really is a long story).

What we find most interesting about the kids' perspectives on our road trips is how little they discuss the actual places that we took them. It is apparent from these thoughts and feelings put on paper that for our little ones, it is not the destination, but the journey they will remember and take with them when they, as Ella so eloquently stated, fly away. Just not too far; we plan to spend plenty of time with our grandkids.

Conclusion

W E SPEND OUR LIVES at top speed trying to make deadlines, get to appointments on time, and get to the front of the grocery checkout line. We are constantly running some sort of race to get the kids packed for school, to find the right camp for summer or to complete our projects at work on schedule. The race we run is ongoing and never ending which is the fun: life's journey. Sometimes as we race together as a family, we can lose track of the time we have with each other.

Before we realize it, the kids we are working so hard to provide for will have lives of their own; their own races and their own families to raise. Our road trip vacations give us a chance to pause the insanity life sometimes offers us. We sit in our car with our young, captive audience and learn more about them and each other in a week then we do in months of extracurricular activities, late work days and hurried family dinners.

As you go on your journeys with your own families, remember there is plenty to discover out there in the diverse and amazing United States. There are monuments built by men and women and natural wonders carved by time. There are theme parks and themed cities and amazing, one-of-a-kind finds in every state. We hope that you too will find the best adventures of your lives on the road with your kids. Happy trails!